THE LAST ARAB JEWS

The Communities
of Jerba, Tunisia

SOCIAL ORDERS

A Series of Monographs and Tracts

Edited by Jacques Revel and Marc Augé,
Ecole des Hautes Etudes en Sciences Sociales, Paris

Additional volumes in preparation

ISSN: 0275-7524

THE LAST
ARAB JEWS

The Communities of Jerba, Tunisia

Abraham L. Udovitch
Princeton University

and

Lucette Valensi
Ecole des Hautes Etudes en Sciences Sociales

Photographs by
Jacques Pérez

harwood academic publishers
chur   london   paris   new york

Published under license by OPA Ltd. for Harwood Academic Publishers GmbH

Harwood Academic Publishers

Poststrasse 22
7000 Chur
Switzerland

P.O. Box 197
London WC2N 4DL
England

58, rue Lhomond
75005 Paris
France

P.O. Box 786
Cooper. Station
New York, NY 10276
United States of America

Published simultaneously in French under the title
Juifs en Terre d'Islam: les communautés de Djerba
by Editions des Archives Contemporaines.

Library of Congress Cataloging in Publication Data

Udovitch, Abraham L.
    The Last Arab Jews.

    (Social orders; v. 1)
    1. Jews—Tunisia—Jarbah Island.   2. Jarbah
Island (Tunisia)—Ethnic relations.   I. Valensi,
Lucette.   II. Title.   III. Series.
DS135.T72U36   1983   306'.0899240611   83-6109
ISBN 3-7186-0135-4

ISSN: 0275-7524   ISBN: 3-7186-0135-4

Printed in Great Britain by Bell and Bain Ltd., Glasgow.

Preface to the Series

The purpose of the social sciences is to develop a clearer comprehension of the contemporary world. In social phenomena, they strive to uncover orders, relationships and levels of organization which, at the same time, define systems of understanding. The social sciences do not impose these systems upon our perceptions arbitrarily, but rather they seek to construct them by the posing and testing of hypotheses in a tentative, step-by-step manner. In order to grasp the meaning of social orders, social scientists draw upon the experiences and methods of various fields, regardless of disciplinary boundaries: the anthropologist, the historian, the economist and the sociologist are united by the common task of redefining objects of study.

The goal of **Social Orders** is to shed light on this intellectual workshop by publishing the recent results of current research in the social sciences.

The Editors

Contents

Acknowledgments

Since beginning our research in 1979, we have incurred debts of gratitude to numerous persons and institutions. Not all can be mentioned here.

Our most profound debt is to the residents of Hara Kebira and Hara Sghira whose good will and generosity were indispensable to understanding their way of life.

We wish also to thank the municipal authorities of Houmt Souk and the Director of the Centre d'Etudes et de Recherches Economiques et Sociales in Tunis, Dr. Bouhdiba, for help extended to us during our research.

Our work was supported in part by the Committee on Middle Eastern Studies of the Social Science Research Council, the Research Committee in the Humanities and Social Sciences of Princeton University and the Délégation à la Recherche Scientifique, Ministère de l'Education Nationale, Paris. We are grateful for their assistance.

A number of colleagues and friends have read and commented on various drafts of this text. Among them, we express our special thanks to Mark Cohen, Grace Edelman, Andras Hamori, Jacques Revel and Abdelkader Zghal.

We are grateful to Mss. Judy Gross and Dorothy Rothbard for their dedicated efforts in typing the English version of this book.

A. L. U. - L. V.

In memory of Denis

Preface

A complex set of intellectual and biographical concerns led us to a study of the Jewish communities of Jerba. Neither of us is a specialist in Jewish history or Jewish studies. We are general historians of the Middle East and North Africa — one a medievalist and the other a modernist — with a specialty in social and economic history and an interest in combining the concerns of social science with those of history.

While all other Jewish communities of North Africa disappeared, those of Jerba resisted both assimilation and migration to become "the last Arab Jews." Why? How were they able to maintain and reproduce their institutions, to adjust to radically changing circumstances while preserving intact their religious and communal identity? Answers to these questions, it seemed to us, might tell us a great deal about the nature and role of ethnic groups in North Africa and in the Arab world, both now and in the past. Studying, in the context of this small group, the close interconnection of ethnicity, religion, economic and social life held the promise of revealing patterns and insights that might be applicable to many other groups in the Middle East and North Africa and to other periods of this region's history. The paradox of a community which was at once so intensely and completely Jewish and at the same time culturally so thoroughly embedded in its Muslim, North African environment promised to tell us something important about both Jews and Muslims and about their interaction in the present and in the past.

These were some of the historical concerns which instigated our research on the Jews of Jerba — a research which demanded the methods of the historian and the anthropologist. As historians we were under no constraints, except those naturally and inevitably imposed by the nature of our source material. This was not at all the case with respect to our fieldwork; here we were caught by the indigenous system of group dynamics.

We strongly felt that properly to understand the Jewish communities of Jerba in their interaction with the surrounding Muslim environment required a double perspective — a view from the inside outward and from the outside inward. However, working within the Jewish community and gaining the confidence of its members virtually excluded the possibility of crossing ethnic boundaries to do the same among the neighboring Muslims.

Given the local conditions, we were unable to situate ourselves at the contact points between the two groups. We ardently hope that other scholars will one day come along to complement our study by taking up a position symmetrical to the one that circumstances imposed upon us.

Jerba requires a novelist or a poet. Only someone with the gift of an Isaac Bashevis Singer could do justice to the tale of Baba Gagou who came from Gabes each year to spend the spring and summer in Jerba. Poor and nearly blind, he survived on the charity of the inhabitants of Hara Sghira, the Small Village, who brought him his meals each day. Dar Zohra, the dwelling he shared with the village idiot and an unmarried madwoman, became the meeting place of the young girls of the village who stopped by each evening to feed these paupers.

Baba Gagou loved to sing. He would launch a melody and the girls would quickly gather around him, responding with a refrain, clapping their hands as they closed the circle and quickly stepping back as soon as they got too close to him. After each song, he insisted upon a rest. And when the young ladies would importune him for yet another song, he would protest that he was tired, that he was "*fragile, delicat*" — using a few of the French words he had picked up in the course of his wanderings.

Baba Gagou could barely see; he smelled of urine and wore ill-fitting hand-me-downs, the largesse of one or another of the local families. During the day, he made the rounds from house to house, talking, telling stories, inquiring into the meaning of life. He spoke of love and death.

Death was no stranger to him; he had already encountered it. One day, as he was out with a poor friend foraging for something to eat, they were attacked, beaten and left for dead. But God was not yet ready to gather him in and Baba Gagou was returned to life.

As for love, he never knew it. He despaired of ever meeting a woman who would love him as his mother had loved him. Why this fate, he would ask? Wherefore this life without love? And what will the next world be like?

It would take a raconteur like Sholem Aleichem to tell the story of the chicken seller of Hara Kebira, the Large Village. He could be seen gesticulating in the market and in the streets from morning till evening, talking, arguing and shouting in the same tones as his chickens. With his thick, horn-rimmed spectacles, he looked like a dishevelled intellectual who had spent the entire night working and studying. In fact he probably spent the night squabbling with his wife. His marriage was an adventure unto itself. A wedding was being celebrated between a woman of Hara Kebira and a man of Hara Sghira. The festivities had begun on a Tuesday and — as was customary — had been going on for almost a week. The bride was about to be led to the house of her groom for the culmination of the ceremony of the "seven blessings" which would consecrate the marriage when, lo and behold, a new law was promulgated prohibiting polygamy throughout the realm. The groom, as it turned out, already had another wife. What to do with the poor bride? She was well past the usual age of marriage, otherwise her family would never have agreed to accept a man from Hara Sghira. And what about the festivities, could one leave them suspended and unconsummated?

This complicated issue agitated the entire community until it was finally agreed to leave it to the local musician to find a way out of the muddle. The poor musician criss-crossed the village in search of an idea and of a substitute groom. His thoughts finally turned to this unsightly young man, without a penny to his name, at least twenty years younger than the waiting bride but sure to have a hard time, now or later, finding any other match.

In a matter of hours, he was fixed up with a brand new suit. With the help of a little money, he was persuaded to overlook the age difference between himself and his future bride, the irregularity of the situation, as well as everything else.

The marriage was celebrated and consummated forthwith. The couple produced several children but the screeching of his chickens never succeeded in drowning the noise of their squabbles.

The sorrows of Sibiya would be a theme suitable for a ballad maker. One couplet would tell of her beauty, the second of how ten young men asked for her hand in marriage and the third of how her family always had a good reason to reject them.

The ballad would tell how Sibiya ended up accepting a man from Gabes, how her father and grandmother perished in an accident on the way to convey her acceptance, and how this marriage never took place. The plaint would tell of the silence and the sorrow in the home and of the years spent in mourning.

After the years pass, one could again sing of the marriage of Sibiya. This time it was to a school teacher. He came all the way from the United States to marry her. The wedding was a grand celebration and everyone helped to prepare her for the voyage to America. But she needed a passport, a visa and many papers which took a long time to get. Her husband had to go back. She had to remain. Letters from him arrived and then they stopped.

Abandoned by her husband, Sibiya took the airplane all the way to Miami to try to convince him to act wisely. He refused to see her or even to speak with her and she returned home to Jerba.

On the day that Sibiya received her divorce document, the air was heavy and the sky was somber. Her entire body trembled and she shut herself up in her room. "Dear God, give me the strength to cross over to the other side. Dear God, carry me off to Your eternal city."

When Sibiya left, the sky was clear and the air light. Her face had the glow of the moon in its fullness.

What follows is neither a novel nor a poem but a description of the Jews of Jerba. The two villages which they occupy could pass virtually unnoticed, so closely do they resemble the other Tunisian villages of the region.

Hara Sghira, set in a landscape of olive trees and orchards is the more continental of the two. It is a village turned inward towards its shaded alleyways, silent and remote — even from the pilgrimage synagogue of the Ghriba to which it is organically connected. About half a mile separates the village from the synagogue. Yet any visitor to the latter — an obligatory stop in any tour of the island — can remain totally unaware of the existence of the former. Hara Sghira, also called Dighet, contains almost 300 Jewish inhabitants.

Hara Kebira, the larger of the two settlements, is closely tied to the market town of Houmt Souk, located almost a mile away. The flow — back and forth — of vehicles and persons of every description between the village and the market town is continuous. More than 800 Jews live in Hara Kebira. It hums with activity from early morning till sunset. Only the relentless light of mid-day slackens the movements of its inhabitants.

These two communities are said to harbor the most ancient Jewish settlements of North Africa. Until very recently, the Maghreb counted numerous communities of the same type and the same importance. For the most part, they have passed out of existence without ever having been described. Small centers of Jewish population continue to exist in places like Tunis or Casablanca. All the others have disappeared or are about to disappear.

Hara Kebira and Hara Sghira also knew better times. At their height, in 1946, the combined population of these two villages numbered almost 4,500 — all of them Jewish. Successive waves of emigration have reduced their numbers. Muslim families have moved in to the space previously occupied by Jews. Nevertheless, and despite their reduced numbers, the Jewish inhabitants of the two Haras have preserved a communal existence.

Hara Kebira and Hara Sghira testify to a multi- secular history. To sketch their portrait is also, in a certain way, to do the same for the other communities of North Africa. In the evocation of various practices and events, many will recognize traits already observed among the Jews of Tiznit, of Ghardaia or of Tlemcen before their departure from North Africa. In this sense, the communities of Jerba emerge as a repository of a vanished culture. Nevertheless, they also possess an unquestionable individuality which explains why they have resisted so long and why, in spite of the serious drain of emigration, they have still not exhausted the possibilities of maintaining and reproducing their cultural identity.

It is this aspect of their existence that this book explores by observing the speech and the gestures of the Jews of Jerba, by scrutinizing their communal life, their interaction with their Muslim neighbors, as well as by a careful look at their long history.

1
A Long History

Embroidered fabric which protects the Torah case.

Myths of Origin

For the Jews of Jerba, their past is as relevant and immediate as their present. An inseparable amalgam of time, space and community constitutes the context of their existence. Their shared past gives shape to their cultural identity and self-perception.

Within the community and among the other inhabitants of the island, a general consensus reigns about the antiquity of the Jewish settlements and the uninterrupted Jewish presence in Jerba. In the indigenous chronology, the Jewish settlement antedates the coming of Islam; it antedates the hegemony of the Romans; it antedates the destruction of the second Temple in 70 A.D. and possibly even the destruction of the first in 586 B.C. On some level, Jerba is perceived as the original and first diaspora. In spite of this consensus regarding its antiquity, there is, surprisingly, no single, recognized version of the community's myth of origin. There are many versions which, even when not mutually contradictory, differ in detail and chronology. Nevertheless, they all make the same statement and have the same meaning.

The most popular account dates the first Jewish settlement in Jerba to the aftermath of the destruction of the Temple of Solomon in 586 B.C. A group of priests (*kohanim*)[1] serving in the Temple escaped from Jerusalem and found their way to Jerba, carrying with them a door and some stones from the Jerusalem sanctuary. These were incorporated into the "marvellous synagogue" (*Ghriba*) which they erected in Jerba, and it is on account of its antiquity and of its connection with the holy Temple of Jerusalem that the Ghriba was and continues to be a locus of pilgrimage and veneration. The priestly refugees from Jerusalem settled in a village nearby this new sanctuary and were the founders of Hara Sghira, also known as Dighet, a supposedly Berberized form of the Hebrew *delet*, meaning door. Until recently, the town was said to be populated only by kohanim, members of the priestly caste descended directly from those who fled Jerusalem in the sixth century before the common era. While the oral form of this tradition probably dates back many centuries, its earliest appearance in written form is apparently that found in a book, *Hashomer Emet*, by Rabbi Abraham Haim Addadi of Tripoli, published in Livorno in 1849.

Other accounts place the origins of the Jewish settlement in Jerba at an even earlier date, contemporary with the first Temple, or even preceding it. Joab ben Zeruyya, one of King David's generals who battled the Philistines, is supposed to have pursued them as far west as Jerba (even further west according to some accounts) and to have founded the Jewish settlement on the island. A stone with an inscription bearing this general's name is said to have been in existence as late as the early 19th century. Still another account attributes the earliest Jewish presence in Jerba to the seafaring Israelite tribe of Zevulun which, at the time of King Solomon, sailed westward and settled on the North African coast in the same manner as did the ancient Phoenicians. Other traditions hold that it was priestly refugees not of the first but of the second Temple (70 A.D.) who were the first Jewish settlers on the island.

Various archaeological artifacts — inscriptions, gravestones, remnants of ancient synagogues, genealogies engraved on stone — which were said to offer material proof for one or another of these myths of origin are now lost and survive only as part of an oral tradition. Local residents also point to certain practices peculiar to the Jews on the island as evidence of the antiquity of Jerban Jewry. For example, the *kiddush*[2] prayer on the eve of Passover, and some of the Prophetic passages on certain Sabbaths of the year are shared with very few other Jewish communities, such as those in Yemen and Tafilat of Morocco and might, therefore, antedate the standarization of Jewish ritual practices.

For the Jews of Jerba themselves as well as for those trying to understand their community, knowing the exact date of their arrival on the island is not of crucial importance.

The significance of the various versions of their beginnings (and there are a number of others not mentioned here) lies not in their chronology. What counts is the symbolic topography outlined by these legends. They situate the Jews of Jerba primarily as part of the Jewish people and, within this broad circle of identity, assign them an honorable place — a direct connection to the Holy Land, to the Holy City and to the Holy Temple. The special status derived from this connection extends not only to the people but also to the place. In the Ghriba there is an element of the authentic Temple. Jerba is the "antechamber of Jerusalem" and, in the opinion of some of its rabbis, is even part of the religious jurisdiction of Jerusalem.

At one and the same time, these legends confer upon the Jews of Jerba the brevet both of authenticity and of antiquity. They are a way of saying: We Jews were here before all the others. In other terms, they assert unequivocally the legitimacy of the Jewish presence on the island. Rationalizing this vision, one learned Jerban Jew maintains that before converting to Islam, all the inhabitants of the island were originally Jewish. In support of his thesis, he points to the survival of certain "Jewish" practices — such as the lighting of a candle on Friday night, or the suspending of *matzot* (the unleavened bread of Passover) from the ceiling from one spring to the next — among a number of Muslim Jerban families.

The accounts of their origins thus constitute a sociological charter, a kind of social contract, rather than a historical document. Claims to antiquity and authenticity in almost identical forms are to be found in other communities. Was not Ghardaia, in the Mzab, considered the second Jerusalem by its Jewish community? Or Tlemcen, where one of King David's generals also halted his westward advance? Or Ifran in Morocco, whose Jews claimed to have left the East at the time of Nebuchadnezer and who called their village "the little Jerusalem"?

Paradoxically, these legends, by placing the Jews in North Africa as Palestinian exiles, profoundly mark them as authentic Maghrebis. Indeed, the correspondence with the accounts of origin of other segments of the society is almost total. Every tribe, every village claims a common origin for itself, postulates a collective migration and settlement in the distant past, and leans heavily on this "history" to define its identity and its position. Furthermore, is not the Jerban tradition a Jewish variant of the myths of origin so common among Muslim maraboutic groups? The latter frequently posit a tie to a symbolic, sacred space, the cradle of the tribe, and assert a claim to a sharifian descent ultimately connecting them to the family of the Prophet. In this respect, the Jewish kohanim of Dighet are comparable to the Muslim *shorfa*. Thus, from this very first feature of their culture one observes a remarkable bond. That which makes the inhabitants of the two Haras Jewish also makes them, in an inextricable manner, North Africans.

Historical Fragments
from Antiquity to the Eighteenth Century

The question, nevertheless, persists. Since when is the Jewish presence attested in Jerba? Does history confirm or deny these legends?

As far as we know, there is not a single vestige — archaeological, epigraphical or literary — relating to the Jews of Jerba during the period of antiquity. At the beginning of this century, some travellers thought they recognized the remains of a synagogue among the Roman ruins of El-Kantara at the southern tip of the island. This identification required a considerable leap of the imagination. Nahum Slouschz, a Jewish scholar who made several trips through North Africa in the early 1900's, contended, as did other experts, that before the advent of Islam, the Berbers of the region had all been Judaized. However, neither Slouschz nor anyone else has yet succeeded in providing convincing proof in support of this hypothesis. It is plausible to posit a Jewish migration from Palestine toward the West after the destruction of

Figure 1: Letter by Isaac, a Jerban refugee, October 1136

the first Temple. That such a migration occurred after the fall of the second Temple is a well-documented historical fact. We know also that in the 4th century A.D., before the Byzantine conquest of North Africa and the persecutions associated with that event, Jewish settlements formed a continuous chain stretching from Egypt to Mauretania. Jerba was perhaps one link in this chain.

The first reliable, dated information concerning a Jerban Jew derives from a document of the eleventh century. This document, as well as several others found in the Cairo Geniza,[3] proves that although an island, Jerba was not isolated from the major historical movements which affected the southern shore of the Mediterranean.

In a business letter written around the year 1030 we read of a certain Abu al-Faraj al-Jerbi who maintained a residence in Qayrawan — the Tunisian capital of the time — and who was active in the trade with the East, i.e., Egypt and the Indian Ocean. From approximately the same period, in any case before 1060, we have a letter addressed to a certain Khalaf ibn Farah ibn al-Zerbi, who was temporarily in Egypt, but whose arrival was expected both in Sicily and in Qayrawan. In September, 1060, a Tunisian merchant writing from Al-Mahdiyya to his business associate in Old Cairo (Fustat) says: "I sent you a bag of coins containing 70 gold dinars . . . carried by a Jew from Jerba (*bi-yad al-yahudi al-jerbi*). This sum represents the price paid for the flax which I sold." In 1107 another Jerban Jew appears on a list of needy persons who were receiving assistance (in this case, free clothing) from the community in Old Cairo. Toward the middle of the 12th century the information on Jerba in the Geniza documents is entirely concerned with the Jewish captives taken during the Norman raid on the island in 1135. These were apparently quite numerous. A letter from October 14, 1136 speaks of the arrival in Alexandria of a ship containing the Jewish prisoners from Jerba. One of these captives, who was apparently brought to Egypt by his Norman captors and ransomed with money donated by members of the Egyptian Jewish community, has left us a fragment of a highly interesting letter, the earliest first-person testimony by a Jew from from Jerba (fig. 1). Writing from Tripoli in Libya to his benefactor in Cairo, the writer signs his letter as "Isaac, the son of Rabbi Sadaqa, the cantor, a captive from among the captives of Jerba." In this letter he describes the difficult circumstances which befell the members of his immediate family (father, brothers, nieces) who were living in Tripoli. It is not clear whether this Isaac the cantor was a native of Jerba whose family found refuge in Tripoli, or whether he was from Tripoli and was merely working as a cantor in one of the communities of the island when the Normans arrived. In any case, his sojourn in Jerba was a fateful one for him.[4]

Thus in the first half of the 11th century the Jewish settlement in Jerba emerges as a well-established community, probably of some antiquity. Its members were swept up in what has been called "the commercial revolution" of the 11th century Mediterranean world. Jerban Jews were actively engaged in a trade that extended from Spain through Tunisia and Sicily to Egypt, and beyond to South Arabia and India. They were part of an international commercial network which associated them not only with their coreligionists — Jewish merchants from Tunisia and Egypt — but also brought them into contact with Italian traders from Amalfi, Genoa and Venice, who were just beginning to venture across the Mediterranean in search of North African and Eastern commodities. We find Jerbans settled — at least temporarily — in Qayrawan, Cairo and Sicily. In the early 11th century, the Jews of Jerba already exhibited the geographic mobility which was to remain characteristic of this community in subsequent centuries. Neither then nor later did the waters surrounding the island separate its Jewish inhabitants from the goings-on in the outside world. Then, as later, the destiny of the Jewish communities of Jerba was determined not by its isolation from, but by its own particular mode of interaction with the prevailing trends in its Jewish, North African and general milieu.

Of the internal life, culture and mores of the Jews of Jerba in medieval times, we have but a single piece of evidence. It is from the pen of Maimonides (1135-1205), the greatest intellectual figure of Judaism under Islam, and it is not in the least flattering. In a letter of advice to his son Abraham, Maimonides has the following to say about the Jewish populations of southern Tunisia and Tripolitania:

> You should also be aware of certain people who live in the western region called al-Zirbi, i.e. localities in the countries of Barbary, for they are dull and coarse. And you should always be extremely cautious of the people who live between Tunis and Alexandria in Egypt and who also live in the mountains of Barbary, for they are more stupid in my opinion than other men, although they are very strong in faith; God is my witness and judge that in my opinion they are like the Karaites, who deny the Oral Law; they have no clear brain at all, neither for dealing with the Bible and the Talmud nor for expounding *aggadot* (nonlegal portions of rabbinic writings), and *halakhot* (rabbinic laws). Some of them are *dayyanim* (rabbinic judges) but their beliefs and actions in matters of ritual unclean-ness are like those of the sons of abomination, who are a nation of the nations dwelling in the lands of the Ishmaelites. They do not ever look at the ritually unclean woman at all; they do not regard her figure or her clothes, they do not speak to her and forbid walking upon ground her foot has trodden. They do not eat of the hind quarter of animals, and many more and longer stories may be told of them, their customs and their doings.[5]

In spite of Maimonides' harsh, unsympathetic portrayal of the Jews of Barbary (especially those called "al-Zirbi") we do learn something from this account about the culture and institutions of Jewish Jerba and its neighboring communities. Already at that time, i.e., the late 12th century, there were local dayyanim and the study of the Talmud and other rabbinic texts was pursued there, albeit not in a manner of which the great master of Fustat approved. While we do not know how widespread the familiarity with these texts was at that time, we can now at least be reasonably sure that the study of advanced rabbinic texts in Jerba has been continuous since the 12th century, and that this study produced generation after generation of local dayyanim and other religious specialists of various levels and quality of learning.

Their preoccupation by early medieval times with purity in sexual and dietary matters is striking on a number of counts. Various later observers of the Jerban Jewish community have come away with a very similar impression concerning the prominence of its concern for ritual purity. While this may indicate a rather fascinating and unusual continuity of style and emphasis in religious practice for seven or eight centuries, it also reflects a much more fundamental quality of Jerban Jewish life, one which Maimonides himself comments on. "Their beliefs and actions in matters of ritual uncleanness," he reports, "are like those of the sons of abomination, who are a nation of the nations dwelling in the lands of the Ishmaelites." Maimonides is here referring to the Ibadis, a sectarian Muslim group, which until the 20th century formed the majority population of the island of Jerba. This judgment concerning the Ibadis and their exaggerated attention to ritual cleanliness is confirmed by the Arab geographer al-Idrisi writing about the same region at approximately the same time:

> They believe that their clothes become unclean through contact with those of a stranger; they do not extend their hand to a stranger nor do they eat with them or offer them food except in utensils kept specifically for this purpose. Men and women purify themselves every morning. Before every prayer, they make their ablutions and also cleanse themselves with sand. If a traveller draws any water from one of their wells, they drive him off and remove all the water from that well. Clothes of a ritually impure person are not allowed to touch those of a ritually clean person and *vice versa*.[6]

Both Maimonides and al-Idrisi were struck by the particular style adopted by the Muslims and Jews of this region. While the prescriptions on sexual and dietary matters are the same for Jews everywhere, those of Jerba chose to amplify and elaborate their implications. And, while the requirements of ritual purity of the Ibadi Muslims differed substantially from those of the Jews, their shared aversion to impurity led both groups to isolate themselves in order to avoid any corrupting contact. This common preoccupation has given the culture of both groups a local coloration, which has persisted to the present.

This penchant to magnify the slightest aspects of religious life has remained a distinctive feature of Jerban Judaism. Each practice is saturated with supererogatory elements deriving from a profound interaction with its local and regional milieux.

For the 600-year period from approximately 1150 to 1750, all the testimonies concerning the uninterrupted Jewish existence in Jerba are from sources external to the island and the community. None of the major events which overtook the island and the community left any trace in its oral and written memory. As momentous an upheaval as the anti-Jewish persecutions by the Almohads in the late 12th century is known only from a brief reference in a medieval Hebrew poem. From it, we learn that Jerba, together with other small communities of southern Tunisia (Gafsa, Al-Hamma), was subjected to a fate of forced conversion and temporary exile:

> And why, Rabbi Avram, have you forgotten some communities?
> You mentioned neither the city of Al-Hamma, nor Gafsa, nor Jerba
> Which perished in the fullness of their exile.[7]

By the early 13th century, the Jews were reestablished on the island, and from Latin sources we learn that in 1239 a group of Jews from Jerba settled in Palermo, Sicily, then under Norman rule. In Palermo, they are said to have constituted a community distinct from the other Jewish inhabitants of that city and to have obtained special concessions from Frederick II for the cultivation of henna and indigo. They also served for some years as royal tax-farmers to the Norman king. We do not know why or how these Jerban Jews came to Palermo; however, it is significant that while there they kept themselves apart from the other Jews — apparently in order to practice and preserve their specifically Jerban religious customs. It is also quite likely that they continued to maintain familial and other ties with their home community.

It is primarily in the context of their connections with the other parts of the Islamic Mediterranean world that the Jews of Jerba appear in the rabbinic *responsa* (legal consultation) literature. Rabbi Shim'on Duran (1361-1444), the chief rabbi of Algiers, was consulted about the validity of a bill of divorce which was to be executed in the Algerian city of Bejaya. One of the parties to this unsuccessful marriage — apparently the husband — was from Jerba. A generation later, Rabbi Shlomo Sarur describes an inquiry from Jerba concerning a partnership between two Jerban Jews who were active in the export of oil and woolens from Jerba to Egypt. One of the partners was struck down by an epidemic while trading in Egypt and all of his property was confiscated by the local authorities. The second partner subsequently died, and the problem posed to Rabbi Sarur related to the complex claims and counterclaims of the heirs to these two deceased merchants.

For the 16th and 17th centuries we encounter several other responsa concerning commercial matters posed by Jerban Jews to rabbis in Tunis, Algiers and Cairo. In the collected responsa of Rabbi Moses b. Isaac al-Ashqar (1465-1540), who was born in Spain and served as a rabbi in Tunis and Cairo, we find the single responsum which tells us something, albeit very generally, about Jewish life in Jerba and about Jewish-Muslim relations in that period. Some Jews owned livestock. On the Sabbath, it was their accepted practice to entrust the care of their animals to Muslim shepherds. This custom was brought into question, since the grazing practices of these non-Jewish shepherds involved a possible violation of the strict rules of observance of the Sabbath rest. The validity of the Jerban practice was sustained by Rabbi Moses. His decision, however, is less interesting than the fact that from this responsum we learn that there were Jewish livestock owners in Jerba in the 16th century, and that, as the text makes clear, a cordial and mutually beneficial level of economic cooperation and division of labor existed between the Jewish and non-Jewish inhabitants of the island.

During the 16th century, Jerba was once again caught up in the swirl of great historical events. In the rivalry between the great empires of East and West, supremacy in the Mediterranean remained the great prize. In 1560, Charles V launched a major expedition against Jerba, and we owe the very first cartographic representation of Jerba to a description of the bloody battle which ensued. Both Jewish villages appear on this map, situated in exactly the same places they still occupy (fig. 2). Apparently the Jewish settlements constituted the only two towns on the island which, according to an Italian description written in 1587: "was settled in its entirety with houses scattered about without order" (*da per tutto habitata con case sparse sanza ordine*).[8]

The Jews were even then recognizable by the clothes which they wore as well as by their headdress. One author of the 16th century wrote: "they are dressed in light purple with a kind of *jebba* (cloak) which reaches down to their knees." Another spoke of: "Jews who are dressed in blue garments and whose heads are wrapped in yellow turbans."[9]

As the center of gravity of world affairs moved westward toward the Atlantic, information about Jerba and its inhabitants became increasingly sparse. During the 18th century, the Jews appear in the fiscal registers of the Beylical government as payers of the *jizya* — the special poll-tax. The obligation to pay this tax flowed from their status as *dhimmis*, a condition they shared with all other Jews in Tunisia and, indeed, with all the "people of the Book" — mostly Christians and Jews — living under Muslim rule. Theoretically, the *dhimma* refers to a permanent, ongoing contract according to which the Muslim ruler conferred his protection on followers of the other revealed religions in exchange for their acceptance of Muslim domination. This protection implied a tolerance for their religion. In return, the payment of the jizya, a tribute already mentioned in the Qur'an (9:29), and which came to correspond to a poll-tax, constituted the primary expression of their subjection. Other conditions of this relationship of protection/domination were defined in the so-called Pact of 'Umar, a document attributed to the second Muslim caliph, and which became a basic text of reference for all Muslim countries. Its provisions regulated such things as the height of non-Muslim houses (not to overtop their Muslim neighbors), restricted the uses of non-Muslim places of worship (no ostentation), forbade dhimmis to ride horses or bear arms and prescribed the specific type and color of the clothes dhimmis were to wear.

The rigor with which these prescriptions were applied varied from one period to another and from one region to another. We do know that the Jews of Jerba continued to pay the special poll-tax and to wear distinctive clothing until these requirements were officially abolished by the promulgation in 1857 of the *Pacte Fondamental*, a charter of basic rights for the Bey's subjects. We do not know whether their residence in the Hara was the result of enforced or voluntary segregation.

Their oral tradition preserves a memory of other restrictions as exemplified by the following story told to us by a young Jerban:

> Once upon a time a Muslim notable offered a horse as a gift to a Jew named Soufir. The Jew was astounded. "What am I going to do with a horse? Jews are not allowed to mount a horse."
> "Take it, nevertheless," responded his benefactor, "and you will see."
>
> And, indeed, Hammuda Pasha soon delivered the Jews from this prohibition. It happened in 1859. The very same Soufir contributed funds for the decoration of the synagogue of Rebbi Brahem and his name is still engraved there on a ceiling beam.

This Soufir did exist and one can indeed read his name on the beam of Rebbi Brahem's synagogue. It was, however, the Bey Muhammad and not Hammuda Pasha who, in 1857, lifted the discriminatory restrictions which weighed upon the Jews.

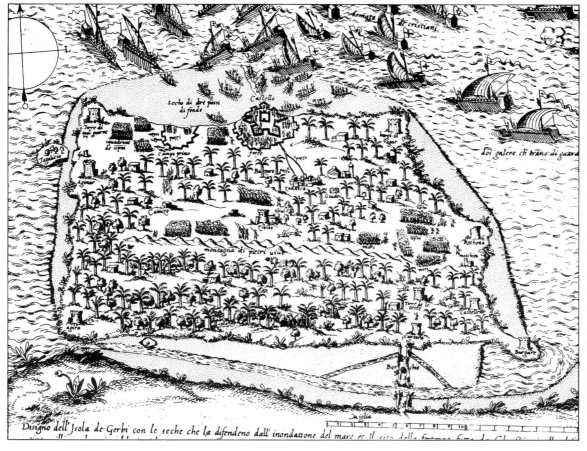

Figure 2: The first cartographic representation of Jerba, 1587.

Another story tells us how Rabbi Shaul Hacohen (1772-1848) was reduced to tears upon learning the news of the emancipation of slaves in Tunisia in 1846. He returned to his home in a state of great distress, fell into a deep sleep and had a dream. When he woke up, he announced in a trembling voice to his anxious and perplexed disciples that the liberation of the Blacks would be followed by the redemption of the Jews. Thus, the abolition of slavery nourished the messianic hopes of Jerban Jews.[10]

Both state and society in Tunisia were non-secular. Since religious rules governed many aspects of life, tolerance in religious matters encompassed large domains of social practice. The purview of religion extended beyond the simple limits of beliefs and observance of rituals and included such domains as education, social welfare, problems affecting personal status, social ethics and even economic practices. The central government collected taxes and assured internal peace and security. Most other aspects of social and public life were left to the communities which enjoyed relative autonomy in these matters. To be born into a certain religious group meant that one was immediately integrated into a given social network, excluded from others and that ultimately, one understood and conformed to the rules which governed the interaction between one group and another. Adherence to a religious group structured the entire range of one's social relations, on the inside as well as on the outside of the community. Traces of this principle continue to be visible in Jerban society to the present.

15

The Jerusalem of Africa

In the indigenous Jerban accounts of the community's history, there is a void between the arrival from Jerusalem and the 18th century. Not a single fact, a single event or a single personality or name fills this span of approximately two millennia.

The second cycle of their historical account begins with the 18th century. By that time, Jerba had emerged as an important center of Jewish learning, comparable to Tunis, and as a highly developed and self- sustaining community. How did Jerba achieve this status? Again, the details are obscure, and will probably remain so, but there is a legend which seeks to account for the intellectual revival of Jewish life in Jerba, in Tunis and Libya. The legend which inaugurates the second cycle of Jerban Jewish history is the mirror image of that describing its origin in antiquity. The new beginning orginated not in the East with refugees *from* Jerusalem, but in the West with pilgrims *to* Jerusalem. The new beginning was not anonymous and vague, but is associated with specific and known personalities and has a continuity and succession to the present day. Throughout, it is filled with actual people and with actual texts, documents and events. The early legend establishes Jerba as the most ancient Jewish community of the diaspora; the later legend contains some elements explaining why Jerba became the last community of the Islamic Jewish diaspora. The ancient myth establishes the link between Dighet and the Holy Land and makes Jerba the antechamber of Jerusalem, while the later legend, centered on Hara Kebira, builds on the first and provides the basis for understanding the emergence of Jerba as a pre-eminent place of traditional learning and uncompromising traditional practice, or, to use the indigenous metaphor, how Jerba became "the Jerusalem of Africa."

The intellectual renaissance of the 18th century is associated in popular history with its contemporary revival in Tunis and Tripoli, and is connected with the names of three learned men from the West: Rabbi Mas'ud al-Fasi, Rabbi Shim'on Lavi and Rabbi Aharon Peretz. According to an account which enjoys widespread currency among the Jews of Jerba, these three men set out from Morocco intending to settle in the Holy City of Jerusalem. None of them, however, reached this destination. As they travelled across North Africa, they observed the neglected state of Jewish religious knowledge and practice in the communities of Tunisia and Libya. Ignorance was so widespread that in some places as common a ritual as the Sabbath prayers was improperly conducted. Each concluded that he could render a greater services to God and His commandments by foregoing a journey to the Holy Land in order to re-establish Jewish religious learning on firm foundations in this region of North Africa. Mas'ud al-Fasi (d.1775) abandoned his journey in Tunis, Shim'on Lavi in Tripoli and Aharon Peretz (d.1766) in Hara Kebira, Jerba. Each of them inaugurated a brilliant period of study and learning in his adoptive community which was to flourish for many generations after them. Only that of Aharon Peretz endures in the same place to this very day.

Historically, the accuracy of this account is flawed in a number of respects; symbolically, however, it reflects a historical process which did indeed take place. The three initiators of this revival were actual historical figures, but were in no way contemporaries. Shim'on Lavi, who sparked the upsurge of Jewish learning in Tripoli, and who was the author of the *Ketem Paz*, an influential commentary on the Zohar, and the composer of Bar Yohai, the most popular religious hymn of North African Jewry, lived almost two centuries before the other two rabbis with whom popular history has associated him. He died in Tripoli in 1585.

As for Aharon Peretz, it is very likely that he was a native of Jerba and not an immigrant from the West. His grandfather, Shlomo Peretz, was mentioned as living in Jerba in the first book published by a Jerban Jewish scholar (Livorno, 1761). In it, Rabbi Ishaq Haddad says that he saw a certain notation "in the copy of the Talmud belonging to the venerable Rabbi Shlomo Peretz." Thus, this early family must have already been established in Jerba by the early 18th century. Furthermore, while the career of Aharon Peretz coincides with a

16

sustained upsurge in Jewish learning in Jerba, our evidence indicates that neither of the two communities on the island was destitute of such learning by the beginning of the 18th century. Aharon Peretz was preceded by several generations of able scholars and surrounded by a number of outstanding contemporaries. The published works of both Ishaq Haddad and Aharon Peretz — works which were composed in the first half of the 18th century — are replete with references to individuals designated as "teachers and rabbis," some of whom are described as already having composed important works of Talmudic and legal commentary (e.g. Rabbis Nissim Khayyat, Abraham Cohen and others). Numerous contemporaries are also mentioned in these works, as are the discussions which took place on various points "in the *yeshiva*," or with members of the *beth din*, the rabbinic court. By the early 18th century, an intellectual upsurge encompassing a significant number of scholars and rabbis in the two communities was well underway.

If these scholars had precursors in the 17th or preceding centuries, we know nothing about them. It should be noted that the discussions and creations of the Jerban rabbis were contemporaneous with a parallel upsurge in traditional learning in the capital city of Tunis whose rabbis were producing and publishing books in growing numbers.[11]

In Jerba, the two "stars" of this revival — Ishaq Haddad and Aharon Peretz — are both said to have come there from the West: Haddad from Algeria or Gibraltar and Peretz from Morocco, probably Fez. Even Dighet — the village of priestly families — has preserved a tradition that some of the families of kohanim there derive not from the original refugees from the destroyed Temple of Jerusalem but from families of much later arrivals from the West. Thus the attribution of its religious upsurge to the arrival of particular individuals from Morocco or Spain, while inaccurate in its details and chronology, contains a kernel of historical truth. The influx and dispersal of Jewish refugees from Spain served as an intellectual catalyst for all the Jewish communities on the Islamic shores of the Mediterranean who received them. In addition, the messianic movement of Sabbatai Zevi was followed by an intensified contact of North African Jewish communities with the religious academies in Palestine in the late 17th century. Emissaries from the rabbinic academies in Safed, Jerusalem, Tiberias and Hebron criss-crossed North Africa collecting funds in support of their institutions located in the Holy Land.[12] Many of these passed through Jerba, bringing with them new ideas, new texts and new knowledge. So, for example, Aharon Peretz, in a work of exegesis and commentary which appeared posthumously in Livorno, mentions fifteen or sixteen such visitors to Jerba by name and attributes to them new ideas and insights.

The early 18th century was a beginning not only intellectually but also institutionally. This was especially so for Hara Kebira. Many of the synagogues of Hara Kebira date from this period or slightly later. None can be securely dated to an earlier period. The beautiful and moving synagogue complex of Sla Rebbi Brahem was established by Abraham Haddad, the youngest son of Ishaq Haddad, the author of the first published work by a Jerban rabbi. The synagogue must have been constructed before the latter's death in 1755 since it contained a separate study for Rabbi Ishaq. This synagogue is in active use to this very day, carefully maintained by the direct descendants of its founder. The Sla Rebbi Hezkiyah was founded by the son of Aharon Peretz in the mid-18th century. The Sla Sghir and the Sla Rabbi Bezalel (severely damaged by arsonists in the summer of 1979) also date back to the same period. The emergence at this time of larger synagogues which were more than just family chapels went together with the growth in each of them of yeshivot — schools for religious training and study. This synagogue-centered system of religious education and study at all levels, which first appears in the mid-18th century, dominated the upbringing of the males of Hara Kebira for more than two centuries until the educational system was reorganized less than two deades ago.

The first evidence of the Jerban predilection for localizing the religious practices they shared with observant Jews everywhere in the world emerges at this time. In the biography of Rabbi Aharon Peretz we are told that, in addition to all his other outstanding qualities as a rabbi and judge, he also instituted (Hebrew: *tiqqen*) a number of local regulations in ritual matters which became customary practices of the community ever since. For example, it was he who forbade the eating of locusts in the two communities of Jerba, a practice considered religiously licit until his time; he established the manner in which the ram's horn (*shofar*) is sounded during the New Year's service. It subsequently became *de rigueur* to include in the accounts of the lives and accomplishments of great Jerban rabbis not only examples of their great learning, piety, humility and charity, but also to enumerate the regulations and local elaborations of the law which they instituted. This talent of adding a specifically Jerban layer to the fence which generations of rabbis and interpreters from all over the world had built around the Torah became a much-prized and admired quality.

No major rabbinic figure in Jerba of the past two centuries has lacked this quality, and its most outstanding representative possessed it in abundance. Rabbi Moshe Khalfon Hacohen (1874-1950) is without doubt the most revered and important rabbinic personage in the modern history of Jewish Jerba. His impact on the community as a leader and scholar was massive and long-lasting. Among his most important achievements was the compilation in four small volumes of all the regulations and local customs of the Jewish communities of Jerba. This collection, entitled *Brith Kehuna* (*The Covenant of Priesthood*), has achieved the status of a law book and has become a standard work of reference and guidance for Jerban Jews. Rabbi Khalfon's compilation was a culmination of a multi-secular process the beginning of which, while it might antedate the 18th century, is first visible at that time.

By codifying their local customs, the rabbis, in effect, concluded a covenant between God and the community. They provided a Jerban anchorage for the universal commandments of the Jewish religion; they established a direct connection between "the Lord Almighty," distant and impersonal, and their own city. God could feel at home in Jerba, just as the Jerban Jews could live in cordial familiarity with the Almighty. At the same time, by ratifying local customs, the rabbis as bearers and guardians of the universal tradition endowed them with legitimacy. Jewish religious practice is based on a double system of *minhag* and *halakha*, custom and law, recalling the *'urf* and *shari'a* of their Muslim neighbors. By setting down in writing the practices specific to their community, the rabbis elevated them to the rank of law and established a continuity between one system and the other. Moshe Khalfon Hacohen is very clear on this point. If the local customs, he asserts, are at variance with the rulings of the *Shulhan 'Arukh* (the authoritative compilation of Jewish religious law), they are nevertheless binding on the Jews of Jerba.

The rabbis laid the foundations for the "theocratic republic" which has persisted to the present. They promoted the corpus of local customs to the status of a charter for the community. As the guardians of both the universal commandments and the local heritage they were able to establish their own authority. In fact, it was during the late 18th and 19th centuries that rabbinic authority increased to the point where it dominated most aspects of public and private life. It succeeded in establishing effective educational and social service institutions and in resisting outside influences.

The nature and meaning of this authority is illustrated by the following story taken from a recent book written by a Jerban scholar:

> The head of the Jerban Jewish community was called "shaykh." We know the shaykh Shmuel (Shmula) Haddad who lived in Jerba at the beginning of the 19th century. He was the brother of Rabbi Nissim Haddad who served as a rabbinic judge together with Rabbi Israel. Among the shaykh's responsibilities was the requirement 'to beat with a stick anyone who violated a religious prescription and was found guilty by the rabbinic court.'
>
> In his time, the following proverb was current: *fi ayyam Shmula al-sha'ira qad al-fula* — in the days of Shmula, the barley was the size of beans. That is to say, because there were few evildoers, there was a great abundance in the land which was enjoyed by all.

18

It is told that when his brother Rabbi Nissim, the judge, used to pass through the market, all the malefactors would flee before him. He used to check whether or not they had performed their prayers and put on their *tefilin* (phylacteries) by examining their arms for the traces left by the leather bands of the tefilin. If he discovered a Jew who had not put on the tefilin that day, he would order his brother to strike him. In the times of these two brothers — the judge and the shaykh — not a single person among the Jews of Jerba dared to trespass any religious precept or to violate the framework of religion and morality.[13]

The authenticity of this account — at least in its essentials — is confirmed by a decree of the rabbinic court of Tunis issued in 1825 which grants the community in Hara Sghira judicial independence from the rabbinic court of Hara Kebira. For some decades, the jurisdiction of the rabbinic court of the larger community extended over the smaller community as well, and included the spheres of personal (marriage, divorce, inheritance), commercial, and, to some extent, even criminal law. Enforcement was harsh, uncompromising and even highhanded; in the words of the decree, offenders were "chastised with rod and whip." A summons "to appear before the beth din of the Hara struck such fear in their hearts that some fled and rebelled against them."[14]

Within the framework of the religious autonomy enjoyed by the community, the extent and effectivenss of the beth din's authority cannot be doubted — no matter how harshly it was applied. The story of the collaboration between Rabbi Nissim Haddad and his brother Shaykh Shmula exemplifies the organic connection between the authority of the rabbi/*dayyan* and the general consensus of the community and the informal way in which the former was imposed and enforced. Individuals formally condemned by the beth din were subject to corporal punishment and, in spite of some dissatisfaction with this system, it was generally accepted and even perceived as contributing to the well-being of the community. It was not, however, explicit coercion which preserved religious standards. It was rather the comprehensive force of the communal consensus which Rabbi Nissim was seen to faithfully represent. Shame and the opprobrium of public opinion were the most potent forces of social control.

This story is paradigmatic in yet another way. It equates the effective reign of rabbinic authority, the absence of evildoers and the adherence of Jews to their religious law, with the prosperity, not only of the pious and righteous, but of the entire community ("the barley seeds were the size of beans"). This type of equivalence is also found among other groups. It does, however, highlight the fact that in Jerba — then as now — individual violations of accepted norms are seen as threatening to the whole society. In the Jerban view of things, individual behavior and collective well-being are part of the same continuum.

Joining specifically local customs to a system of law which is universal, and theoretically immutable, endowing local scholars, saints and pious persons with the role of legitimator of a distant and impersonal God and mediator between his set of commandments and the burden of local culture is one mode which a universalist religion can adopt in adjusting to diverse environments. Christianity and Islam offer many examples of this adaptive process. Most significantly, it is a prominent feature of North African Islam. It is this mode through which local custom was integrated into Islamic religious law and which produced an interlocking system all across North Africa of cults of local marabouts. Throughout of Middle East and North Africa, it inspired a genre of historical writing which centered on the biographies of local scholars and men of religion. Paradoxically, or maybe not, the Jews of Jerba, while engaged in their most Jewish activity — creating and compiling their own religious customs, recounting the lives and accomplishments of their rabbis — were, once again, engaging in a very North African activity.

19

Jerba was not the only Tunisian or North African community which produced remarkable rabbis and scholars in the 18th and 19th centuries, nor was it the only place where the authority of rabbinic courts was vigorously exercised. But only Jerba was able to consolidate and maintain this religious leadership throughout the colonial period and beyond, at the very time when the communal fabric everywhere else was disintegrating. Furthermore, Jerba extended its influence to other regions. In the 19th and 20th centuries, its inhabitants emigrated, enlarging older communities or forming new ones from Gafsa in the West to Benghazi in the East (figure 3). With them, the Jerbans carried their books, their customs and their values. The island exported rabbis and witnessed an impressive expansion of the pilgrimage to the Ghriba. Jerba, thus, became the capital of an archipelago extending from eastern Libya to the south of Tunisia and its religious preeminence was recognized in the north of the country as it was in neighboring Algeria.

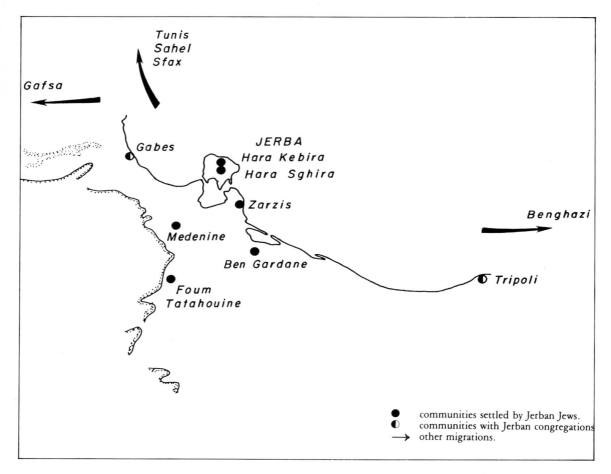

Figure 3: The Jerban Jewish Archipelago.

By contrast, in most other communities the lay and economic elites competed with and succeeded in displacing the religious elites. Religious education, rabbinic authority and the ideology which these represented retreated in the face of secularization and the growing importance of French culture. The social mobility made possible by the advent of colonialism ultimately undermined the traditional framework of the community.

How did this come about? It was neither its insular position nor its distance from large urban centers that made it safe from outside influences. Jerba was subjected to the same pressures as the other communities, particularly in the educational sphere. Its community, however, responded with a coherent and effective two-tiered strategy: an absolute rejection of any form of secular education and a simultaneous strengthening of traditional education. The circumstances of this choice will be explored below.

Were the Jerban communities more homogeneous than those in the rest of the Maghreb? It is true that many of the larger communities were composed of two elements. In many Tunisian cities, Livornese Jews were juxtaposed to native Tunisian Jews. The former led the way in importing cultural models from Europe. In Jerba, a small number of Jewish families, mostly of Italian origin, and connected to large-scale Mediterranean commerce, settled in Houmt Souk in the 19th century. This group, too, was open to western influences. Yet, in spite of their wealth and power — they built the synagogue at Houmt Souk, contributed generously to Jewish projects and, consequently, occupied a prominent position in the community — these merchants were unable to impose their attitudes on the community which remained faithful to its own models.

For many years, the colonial authorities and the Jewish notables of Tunis would characterize Jerba as a "backward" community kept in "abjection and ignorance by their rabbis who were stubbornly opposed to any progress." Far from being ignorant, the Jerbans were offering resistance — at times silent and at times quite vociferous — to any challenge to their own values. The fact that they are still there today proves that, in this particular contest, they prevailed.

1. Arabic or Hebrew words are italicized only at their first occurrence in each chapter. Explanations and definitions are given in the text and are recapitulated in the glossary at the end of the book.
2. Prayer pronounced over wine before the Sabbath and holiday meals.
3. A cache of documents and papers found in the "storage" room of the synagogue in Old Cairo (Fustat). The documents date from the 10th century onward and many are written in Judeo-Arabic.
4. The Geniza documents quoted or cited here are all now found in the Taylor-Schechter collection of the Cambridge University Library: T.S 13J25 folio 9; T.S. K15 folio 13; T.S. 10J15 folio 26. For Jerba in the Geniza douments, consult: S. D. GOITEIN, *A Mediterranean Society* Vol. II, pp. 30, 117; IV, 42, 195, 199.
5. MAIMONIDES, *Iggarot u-Sh'elot u-Teshuvot*, Amsterdam, 1712, p. 3a quoted in H. Z. HIRSCHBERG, *A History of the Jews in North Africa*, vol. 1, Leiden, 1974, p. 165.
6. AL-IDRISI, *Description de l'Afrique et de l'Espagne par Edrisi*, ed. and tr. R. Dozy and M. J. De Goeje, Leiden, 1866, p. 129.
7. Cited in N. SLOUSCHZ, *The Jews of North Africa*, Philadelphia, 1927, p. 222.
8. LANFREDUCCI and BOSIO, "Costa e discorsi di Barberia (1587)", *Revue Africaine*, 66 (1925), p. 419 ff.
9. Text cited in C. MONCHICOURT, "L'Expédition espagnole de 1560 contre l'île de Djerba", *Revue Tunisienne*, 1964, pp. 138-140.
10. Shushan HACOHEN, *Pelei Sadiqim*, Jerba, 1930.
11. David CAZÈS, *Notes bibliographiques sur la littérature juive tunisienne*, Tunis, 1893.
12. H. ZAFRANI, *Les Juifs du Maroc. Vie sociale, économique et religieuse*, Paris, 1972.
13. E. HADDAD, *Shorashim bi-Yehadut Tunisia* (The Roots of Tunisian Judaism), Beersheba, 1978.
14. *Ma'asei beth din,* compiled by Moshe Khalfon HACOHEN, Jerba, n.d.

C

2
Symbols of Identity

A mattress maker from Hara Kebira in traditional festive clothes
conversing with one of the "readers" *(batlanim)*.

Recognizing Each Other

Whether in the crowd at the market of Houmt Souk or among the small groups meandering down the alleyways of the two villages, it does not take very long for an observer to discover that Jerba's population is not homogeneous and that its constituent elements belong to different groups. Take the case of Rabbi Khamus. He is a short, slight man with thick glasses and a long beard. Dressed in white, he is wearing large, billowing oriental trousers which reach just below his knees, a vest over his shirt and a burnous of light wool draped over one of his shoulders. On his head there is the inevitable red *chechia*. All of these are quite ordinary items of traditional Tunisian attire. Yet, one can tell that he is a Jew since he is wearing the chechia toward the back of his head. One can further tell that he is a rabbi or scholar because of his beard and white garb. And, if he were to speak, his accent would reveal his ethnic, religious identity.

On the entire island, and indeed in all of Tunisia one observes these same rules. People recognize each other by a series of external signs which, at the same time, mark their affiliation to a certain group, their exclusion from other groups and, as a consequence, set the form and limits of internal and external communication. For example, it is known that in El-Mai, one of the sub-regions of Jerba, all the inhabitants are fair-skinned, that there never was a black among them and that they slur their words when speaking. In Trifa, on the

From left to right:
a carpenter from
Hara Kebira,
one of the 19 children
of the taxi driver
of Hara Sghira,
a schoolgirl
of Hara Sghira.

24

other hand, they are all blacks, and allegedly descendants of slaves. One can recognize an Ibadi, and even identify the sub-sect to which he belongs; one can recognize which clothing designates which village, who is a Berber-speaker and who an Arabic-speaker.

From this point of view, the Jerban Jews emerge as an ethnic group among the other communities of the island, each having at its disposal for internal and external use an entire array of signs, gestures and words which fashion their identity and govern their interaction with others.

The details of costume are among the main distinguishing features. Like the other inhabitants of the island, the Jews wear either the traditional, indigenous costume, or clothing influenced by Western fashions. In either case, there are several indices pointing to Jewish identity. If they wear the indigenous costume, for example, they place the chechia, like our Rabbi Khamus, well back on their heads, whereas the Muslims wear it forward, much closer to their foreheads. The traditional trousers worn by the Jews are either grey or brown and bordered at the bottom by a black band which, according to them, is a symbol of mourning commemorating the destruction of the Temple. When they wear a turban, which is very rare these days, it too is black. A beard almost always designates a Jew, an educated one to be sure, whereas the moustache generally graces a Muslim face.

These details of the dress code are in no sense obligatory, and some features are even of comparatively recent origin. Until the *Pacte Fondamental* of 1857 which granted them a legal status equal to that of Tunisian Muslims, Jewish males could wear only a dark-colored

chechia. The red chechia is an innovation. However, the manner in which it is positioned on the head remains a distinctive sign which, like the other details of costume, has become an emblem instead of a stigma. It has also become a symbol of authenticity to which many Jews, even those who have adopted Western dress, return during the Sabbath and other religious holidays. The clothes of the past have thus become a kind of ceremonial garb.

Western clothing — trousers, shirt, sweater — can be more equivocal. Younger Jews on Jerba adopted this form of dress beginning in the 1960's, in spite of the resistance from their elders who were especially shocked by the disappearance of the religiously-required head covering. Nevertheless, badges of identity persist such as the gold chain worn around the neck and from which specifically Jewish amulets, or names engraved in Latin or Hebrew script, are suspended.

Jewish women wearing the indigenous costume are recognizable by two distinctive features, the headcovering and the outer garment. Their headgear consists of a bright red bonnet with tresses tied by a ribbon of pink wool and held together by a bow of the same color. The silken *fouta* (cloak) in which they wrap themselves has a pattern different from the cloaks worn by women in other groups. Nowadays, most young women have abandoned the traditional costume. This happened in part because of the initiative of the modernizing director of the girls' school who, toward the end of the 1950's, urged his students to give up the fouta entirely or, at the very least, dispense with it while at school. Even after completing their studies, young women no longer have recourse to the traditional costume except for

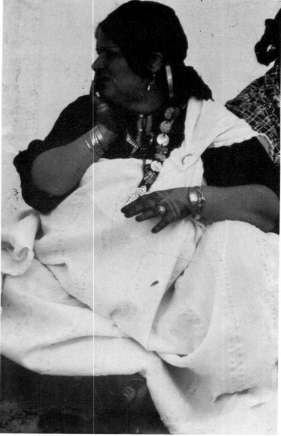

the marriage ceremony. And since Hara Kebira, like all other places in the country, has succumbed to the style of white dresses for brides, it is likely that traditional garments will soon be relegated to the status of folkloric objects in which one dresses up in order to take a souvenir photograph. In their regular, daily lives, women, children and young girls dress in what they call *shuri* dresses — that is, "*à la française*." Only married women still honor the requirement of keeping their hair concealed under a kerchief.

For school-age boys, the indigenous costume has now entirely fallen into disuse, and there remains only one mark of identity, their headcovering. The traditional chechia, which has now become very rare, was replaced by the beret (still visible in photographs of the 1950's) and most recently by a small skullcap of Israeli inspiration which, in order to avoid jeers and harassment, the young boys remove whenever they traverse a Muslim neightborhood.

The borderline between Jews and Muslims marked by their mode of dress is slowly fading and its markers are becoming less obvious. Other differences, however, persist. While the great majority of Jerbans are Arabic speakers, the use of language differs depending on whether one's interlocutors are outsiders or members of one's own group. The Jews have their own distinct accent, a dialect heavily laced with Hebrew words and a discourse interspersed with idiomatic expressions which they share only among themselves. Jewish women, for their part, use a form of speech which their menfolk consider a different language. While these numerous nuances mark differences in gender and status, they do not impede oral communication.

From left to right:
women of Hara Sghira,
at work,
at the door of the Ghriba,
visiting the Ghriba.

27

Written communication, on the other hand, is rendered virtually impossible since, unlike most other Jerbans, the Jews were, until very recently, ignorant of both the Arabic and the French scripts. They write either in Hebrew or in Judeo-Arabic (i.e. a transcription of their Arabic dialectal speech in Hebrew characters). Through the publication of numerous works in their own dialect and in their own local printing presses, the Jews of Jerba have conferred a literary status on a south Tunisian dialect of which these Jewish treatises will, paradoxically, constitute the only written record. In the internal exchange of messages, Jerban Jews do not utilize a universal writing system. While they are acquainted with the modern Hebrew cursive, they continue to prefer the Maghrebi cursive, known as the *ktav sefardi* or as the *m'alaq*. Through a double rejection of any *koine*, Jerban Jews have thus not only distinguished themselves from their immediate neighbors but also from other Jewish groups.

They follow the identical strategy with respect to choosing personal names by clearly distinguishing between males and females, between the ensemble of Jerban Jews and Jews elsewhere, and finally, between Jews and Muslims. For first names, they draw on four major reservoirs of which the most important is the Hebrew Bible. Since the Qur'an retains only a small number of Biblical names, few first names are common to both Jews and Muslims. Where such an overlap does exist, differences in pronunciation leave no doubt as to the ethnic identity of the individual. A Brahem (Jewish) cannot be taken for an Ibrahim, nor a Mushi for a Musa, nor a Yushif for a Yousef. Local Arab words are another significant source for Jerban Jewish first names. While some of these are shared with Muslims (especially such female names as Baya, Urida and Mas'uda), most male Arab first names are used exclusively by Jews and generally have a prophylactic purpose. *Nomen omen*. First names are used as a defense against the two omnipresent dangers of ill fortune and premature death. This preoccupation has given rise to the frequent recourse to fish names (Qarus, Ouzifa), or those based on a variation of the number five (Khamus, Kh'mimes, Khomsana) as well as to the widespread use of prophylactic antiphrases. A newborn child is named Zakino, old man, or Usif, black man. Muslims too share this fear of blind and cruel destiny and they too have recourse to prophylactic practices. These, however, are different varieties of this same species. Names such as Mabruk and Salem are used only by Muslims, whereas Khemais, which in the rest of Tunisia is used by Muslims and Jews is, in Jerba, exclusively Jewish. Thus, a sort of tacit consensus allows each individual a form of ascription to his own group.

Currently, the Jews draw upon yet another onomastic repertory derived from modern Hebrew and imported from Israel. The earliest examples of this category began to appear in the late 1940's as first names for boys, and became widespread in the 1950's. In the case of female names, this innovation came later, and was accelerated by Golda Meir's appointment in the mid-1950's as Israeli Foreign Minister. Since 1967, the use of Israeli-inspired first names for girls as well as boys has become generalized among Jerban families. This was not only a sign of their sympathy toward the State of Israel, but also an expression of their desire to project a different image of themselves. First names are no longer defensive, but connote physical force (Z'ev = wolf, Arye = lion) or symbolic force (e.g. the names of political leaders). There is, perhaps, a further significance to this new choice of names. As the danger and dread of individual death has receded, a desire to defend oneself against collective decline has emerged. The choice of the first name offers a symbolic compensation for one's minority status.

Borrowings from Western languages, principally English and French, constitute the final source of names. Here again, no confusion between the choices made by Muslims and Jews is possible. In Jerba, names such as Dolly or Odette invariably are those of Jews, whereas names such as Sonia and Sami can designate only Muslims. Thus, the decline in the use of purely local first names, and the westernization and change in the choice of names, have taken place in a manner which preserved the parameters of identity and maintained, albeit in an altered position, the ethnic barriers.

It is worth noting the marked asymmetry between the symbolic value the Jews of Jerba attach to male and female names. Just as the modern female costume is "neutral", exhibiting no clear ethnic markers, so too female names are frequently of a neutral western derivation. Male names are most often exclusively Jewish, as if to say that assuring Jewish continuity in the Jerban context is a male task.

Although people do not choose their family names, these unequivocally designate the group to which one belongs. There are, of course, such explicit Jewish names as Cohen and Soufir. But there are in Jerba also Arab names which are borne only by Jewish families, whereas in the rest of Tunisia and in other parts of the Arab world these names are found in Muslim and Christian milieux. In Jerba, the names 'Ammar, Bukhris, Haddad or Houri can designate only Jewish families. The only family name which is shared by both Jews and Muslims is that of Trabulsi which means the Libyan or coming from Tripoli.

As will be described below, the same strategy of identification and voluntary segregation comes into play in many other observable fields of activity. External signs of identity are the subject of a complicated art of physiognomy as practiced by the Jewish and non-Jewish inhabitants of the island. All are in agreement that a person's complexion, hair, look, teeth or the position of the ears are distinguishing physical features indicating ethnic and geographic origins. In the Jerban view, these are associated with character traits and behavior. All of these elements are connected in a manner which implicitly classifies various groups and places them on some hierarchical scale. So, for example, in the eyes of all the inhabitants of Jerba, Muslims and Jews alike, there is a distinct opposition between all Jerbans on the one hand and people from the mainland on the other — the latter being brutal, violent, undisciplined, plundering and dangerous. On the island itself, the population is classified as either Jerbi (Jerban) or 'Arbi (Arab). The Jerbis par excellence are, generally speaking, the town dwellers, even though there were no real towns in Jerba until quite recently. They are town dwellers nonethless by virtue of their urbanity, their language, dress and habitations. The 'Arbi, on the other hand, wears the loose smock and straw hat of the peasant. The groups are endowed with contradictory qualities. The 'Arbi is more rustic, reputedly dirty, and, according to the Jerbi, is to be kept at the threshhold of one's house and not allowed to enter. At the same time, the 'Arbi is associated with the fertility and bounty of the countryside. Transformations are possible. An 'Arbi who became a Jerbi by changing both his place of residence and his costume summed up his change of status by the following nostalgic metaphor: "I was an olive tree; I have become a sterile tree."

The Jews of Jerba divide humanity into two categories: Jews and *Goyim* (non-Jews). On the island, of course, the latter are all Muslims, and they in turn are subdivided along the same lines as those used by other Jerbans. The Jews are totally convinced of their own excellence and of the natural and irremediable inferiority of non-Jews. The Muslims reciprocate with an image which is exactly the inverse. There is, nevertheless, an agreement about certain functional qualities which are recognized as characteristic of the opposite group. Muslims, for example, are held to be good horticulturists, far more skilled than Jews at making an orchard flourish. Jews, for their part, are people of the law. Just as they strictly adhere to the letter of the law of their religion, so too are they punctilious in their transactions. *Haqq al-yahud*, the law and lawfulness of the Jews, is the basis for the trust they enjoy in the economic sphere, especially in the jeweler's trade.

The Jews themselves do not constitute a single, homogeneous group. Rather, they belong to two communities — Hara Kebira and Hara Sghira — the large and small villages. It is not only size which distinguishes between these two settlements, nor is it only the geographic distance of a few miles which separates them. These two villages are at the same time organically connected and structurally opposed. First of all, on the island and even beyond, they occupy two distinct spaces. Hara Sghira is symbolically connected with the East, whereas the inhabitants of Hara Kebira claim a derivation from a migration originating in the West. Each community has its own satellites on the mainland. The communities of Ben Gardane, Medenine and Zarzis were formed by Jews who originated in Hara Kebira, while

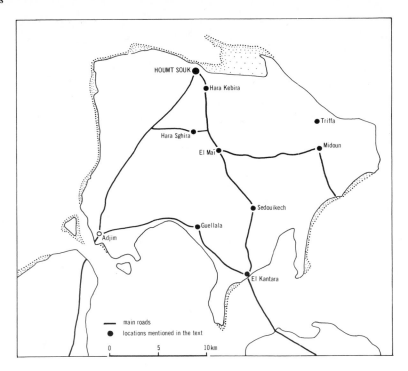

Figure 4:
The Island
of Jerba.

that of Tatahouine was populated by settlers from Dighet. Beyond these settlements, in such places as Gabes or Sfax, Jerbans attached themselves to other groups of Jews, but sooner or later one of the elements would end up as dominant, maintaining affinities with its village of origin. Up until the administrative reforms introduced at the time of Tunisian independence, the colonies created by the migrants from Jerba belonged to two separate jurisdictions. Tatahouine followed the customs of Hara Sghira and submitted to the judgment of its rabbinic authorities, whereas all the others fell into the religious and rabbinic sphere of Hara Kebira. This division of competence was formalized by a responsum of the rabbinic court of Tunis in approximately 1825, one which even at that time appears to have confirmed an earlier practice.

On the island itself, Hara Sghira is associated with the settlements on the southern part of the island such as Guellala and Sedouikech and Hara Kebira with the northern part, most notably Midoun. In a recently published book written by a Jerban Jew, the author asserts, in complete seriousness, that until quite recently, the inhabitants of Guellala practiced cannibalism. Needless to say, the author of the book is himself from Hara Kebira. Hara Kebira, thus, situates itself on the side of culture whereas Hara Sghira is located on the savage side (figure 4). The inhabitants of the former designate themselves as Jerbi whereas those from the smaller villages are called Dightia, which corresponds to the opposition of Jerbi/'Arbi or town dweller/peasant which is prevalent among the Muslims.

Just like other Jerbans, the inhabitants of these villages attribute contradictory qualities to each other. To say of the residents of Hara Kebira that they are more modern is at the same time to cast a slight doubt on their orthodoxy; to say of the residents of Dighet that their community is more ancient, thereby recognizing the authenticity which antiquity confers, is simultaneously to imply a certain archaism, not to say backwardness.

30

Moreover, the males of Hara Kebira do occasionally take their brides from Hara Sghira. The inverse happens but rarely. In Dighet, people complain about the sex ratio being unfavorable to men, while claiming Hara Kebira produces more boys than girls. Thus, one might say that Hara Kebira occupies the masculine pole, that of civilization and high culture, with Hara Sghira situated at the feminine pole, that of nature. Originating from the Holy Land and born into the priestly class, the people of Dighet have something approaching a direct and natural access to God and to the sacred, whereas the inhabitants of the large Hara achieve this by the cultivation of scriptural knowledge.

Even though the relations between the inhabitants of the two villages are somewhat less than friendly, they are indispensable to one another. Just as the Jerbi could not live without the products and labor of the 'Arbi, so are the people of Hara Kebira in need of those of Dighet: their ardent, fecund women, their kohanim and the Ghriba to which the people of both villages render equal homage. Hara Kebira and Hara Sghira form an indissoluble couple.

A Sacred Space

Hara Sghira is surrounded by the *ghaba*, a word which means forest but which in Jerban usage designates a perfectly domesticated countryside. Although the village has five synagogues, not a single one among them is permitted to contain a Torah scroll. These are synagogues from which the ark of the Torah is absent. Three times a week, on Mondays, Thursdays and Saturdays, as well as on the major holidays, the boys and men of Hara Sghira take to the tree-lined road outside the town which leads to the Ghriba. Dighet, thus, lives in symbiosis with the solitary synagogue.

Mondays and Thursdays are market days in Houmt Souk. For Hara Kebira, which breathes to the rhythm of the market, these are days of feverish activity. Before the comparatively recent growth of the town of Houmt Souk, Hara Kebira itself was an important market center. Even now, food stalls and mechanics' shops carry on a permanent business in the village square. Jewelers' workshops line some of the small adjacent streets and can also be found in many of the village's houses. Three rolling mills of near industrial size process gold and silver for the large number of local jewelers. Throughout the entire day, there is a great deal of coming and going at these establishments, with artisans delivering metal to be melted or molded, or simply operating the machines themselves. The chief rabbi of the village runs a printing shop. In former times, there were seven or eight camel-driven mills for grinding cereals. These have now been replaced by electric-powered mills in Houmt Souk.

In the past, circulation between the Hara and Houmt Souk was facilitated by a large number of donkeys, mules and horse-drawn carriages. Today, only a single Jewish coachman is active, and it is he who drives the women to the ritual bath for their monthly *tbila*, or to Houmt Souk, if it is absolutely indispensable that they travel there. There is, also, one last remaining Jewish dealer in mules and horses who sells his animals at the different markets of

31

the island. In the Hara, animals were first replaced by bicycles, then by small motorcycles and, for the more affluent, by automobiles. The mobylette has become the means of transport par excellence and the noise of its motor is a constant accompaniment of village life.

Hara Kebira occupies a territory whose boundaries are traced by a continuous line. A metal wire, like those used to hang laundry in the courtyards of houses, stretches from one rooftop to another all around the town. On the ground, molded reliefs at the foot of the walls of the houses at the edge of the village simulate town gates. This ensemble constitutes the 'eruv, a device which exists in many other Jewish communities as disparate as Toronto and Antwerp. By having an 'eruv, a town situated in a continuous enclosure becomes, for the purposes of religious law, a private domain in which it is permissible for Jews on the Sabbath to carry objects around, something which is otherwise forbidden outside the household space. Here the 'eruv does more than convert public to domestic space. Together with the various other symbols previously mentioned, it contributes to isolating the space and the community in a kind of sacred purity. It delimits an area which is haram, one that is at the same time sacred and forbidden to outsiders. Within the Hara, another wire and other molded reliefs at the corner of the streets which converge on the village square circumscribe the area of the marketplace. As a place of work and of exchange with Muslims, the marketplace is off limits for men on the Sabbath, as it is every day of the week for women. They never cross it, and are obliged to make detours around it when walking from one neighborhood to another. Their lives unfold almost exclusively within the area demarcated by the two lines of the 'eruv.

Beyond the two Haras, the island as a whole seems to share in this quality. How many times does one hear it proclaimed: "Jerba is the antechamber of Jerusalem?" Numerous proofs for this contention are close at hand: the etymology of Dighet, derived from the Hebrew word delet, door, referring to the legend of the fragment of the Temple carried to Jerba from the Holy Land; the healthy climate and the excellence of the island's fruit; the superior quality of the Jerban rabbis of past generations. Even geology is marshalled in support of this legend. The continental drift is transformed into a possible explanation for the island as a broken-off fragment of Palestine.

From a distance, the silhouettes of the two Haras stand out in the landscape. The Muslim population lives dispersed throughout the island. Their residential unit is the individual, semi-autonomous menzel, surrounded by its garden and flanked, in some cases, by a weaving workshop or some other adjunct structure. Even the mosques as places of prayer and assembly were located in isolated spots in the open countryside. Only recently have they become poles around which private houses and public buildings, such as schools, post offices and markets concentrate. Until well into this century, Hara Kebira and Dighet were the only important agglomerations on the island. The flat roofs of the houses trace a series of horizontal lines. Neither cupola nor minaret break the horizon; rather, towering over the other buildings are the cubic masses of the synagogues — eleven in Hara Kebira and five in Hara Sghira — cubes whose walls are pierced by twelve colored glass windows symbolizing the twelve tribes of Israel.

On the inside, the two villages look the same as any quarter of any other traditional village or town in Tunisia — an assemblage of white houses, each one occupied by a single or extended family. Houses are separated by small alleys and passages which are considered and used as private space where it is not not forbidden for women to be seen. The entire area, however, is marked by symbols of Jewish life: the cemeteries on the periphery of the villages; the synagogues and the schools attached to them; the two communal ovens used to keep each family's meal hot on the night between Friday and Saturday. In one open square, people still point to the traces of two olive trees, now uprooted, between which a young bride died one day. This is a spot which young people engaged to be married must always avoid. Then there is the house in which the unleavened bread for Passover is prepared. The Hara has, of course, a ritual bath visited by the women each month after their menstrual

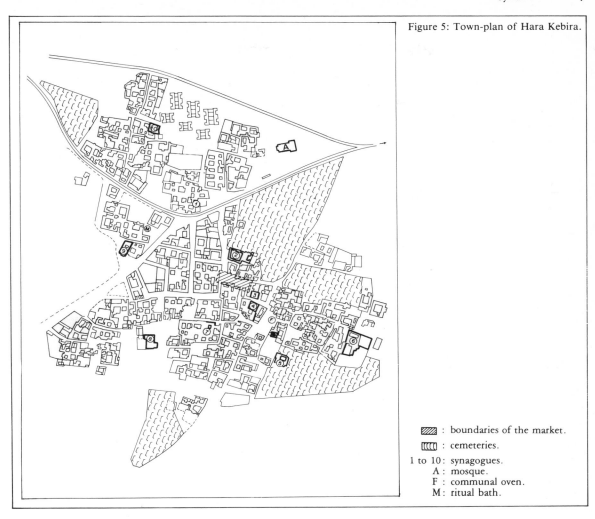

Figure 5: Town-plan of Hara Kebira.

▨ : boundaries of the market.
◫ : cemeteries.
1 to 10: synagogues.
A : mosque.
F : communal oven.
M : ritual bath.

periods, or by prospective brides for the ritual immersion before their weddings. The abattoir in the village square is no longer in use, but there are still butchers' stalls twice weekly providing meat approved by the rabbinic authorities. A vat filled with sand has been built on the side of one of the schools so that the *shohet* will have a place to throw the chickens after slaughtering them (figure 5).

What is true for the villages as a whole is also true for their individual units. At first glance the houses seem like most others in the country. Their large whitewashed walls are pierced by windows with blue borders protected by wrought iron grills. Their placement catches the slightest breeze and ventilates the rooms in all seasons. The entrance is designed so as to block any view of the interior, and rooms are arranged around a central courtyard. Like most other houses, the Jewish residence has its wells and cisterns. The storerooms and the kitchen are grouped on the same side of the house. And, just like menzels of the island, the living quarters or apartments coming off the courtyard have several levels. Symmetrically, coming off the central space shared by all members of the family, there are two elevated alcoves whose floors are covered with mattresses, that of the parents on one side, and that of the children on the other. There is almost no furniture, but several niches and cupboards closed by blue shutters are carved into the walls. A long bench with a stiff back is about the only available seating. Nails of different sizes on every available surface are used to hang tools, utensils and clothes. Factory-made velvet hangings are suspended on the walls, displaying scenes of gardens with fountains, of does and peacocks and, in one case, in a Jewish house, a tapestry depicting Mecca with the Ka'ba at its center.

On the basis of this common Tunisian model, the Jerban Jews created an original variant, a specifically Jewish architecture and decor which simultaneously satisfies their ritual needs and the autarchic familial ideal they cultivate. There is probably no example elsewhere of quite the same degree of correspondence between domestic architecture and the Jewish calendar and Jewish rituals. The important moments of the religious cycle occupy a permanent place in the Jerban house. Symbols of major festivals are visibly preserved in the house until their celebration the following year.

Sabbaths and other holidays are preceded by a ritual bath for all members of the family. Many houses, in both Haras, have a private *mikveh*, a ritual bath sunk into the ground. The women also use the mikveh to purify themselves after menstruation. Right before the Sabbath, and at the beginning of each month, the living render homage to the dead. They light candles in the room where they have their meal, as if the dead returned to the family compound at the most solemn moments of the week and of the year.

Each family has a winepress and a number of enormous jars to contain the wine needed to consecrate each Sabbath and each festival. In the autumn, all members of the family participate in making the wine. Near the winepress stands a trellis from which ripened fruit is hung to dry so that it can be ground, stored and later consumed during the Passover holiday. The autumn cycle, therefore, announces that of the springtime. In some cases, an entire room is devoted exclusively to the dishes and utensils which are used only at Passover. A piece of unleavened bread is preserved, and kept in the house until the following Passover. Finally, a permanent space is reserved for the festival of *Succoth*. This consists of a room with no roof, under the open sky, located either on the level of the other rooms, or else at the corner of the house, slightly elevated and overlooking the courtyard. As Succoth approaches, the opening is covered with palms, and silk fabrics are stretched over the walls. The seat of the prophet Elijah is set down in the room, and on it is placed a copy of the *Zohar*. Succoth, the festival of the gathering of the harvest, here becomes the festival of God's messenger who will announce the arrival of the Messiah and the end of exile. Once the holiday is over, the room remains the same, open to the sky, as if every Jewish family in Jerba always remained ready to greet the awaited prophet. The messianism of the Jerban Jews, which also recurs in their books and their songs, is thus inscribed in the space of their houses. This is the family temple, and this is where the continuity of time is engraved together with the continuity between the living and the dead who await resurrection.

The *mezuzot*, where the *shema' Israel*[1] is written on parchment, protect the threshhold of the house, as well as the entrance to each of its hallways and each of its apartments. This practice is common to Jews all over the world. But the Jews of Jerba add to it an inexhaustible array of prophylactic objects. Against scorpions, they add a bulb of garlic with seven cloves, a pod with seven beans, and an olive branch gathered at the Passover season; or they suspend on their doors a magical text dictated by their rabbis and written by schoolboys seven weeks after Passover, at the *Shavu'oth* season. Against the evil eye, they hang a necklace of various amulets on the wall, and paintings or sculptures of hands guard the doors. Throughout North Africa, the fish, like the hand, is considered an effective talisman against ill-fortune. Fish appear in many guises. Fishtails and fish teeth, or else chains of little fish are dried and hung over the entrance to houses. Fish are found in embroidery, as cast statues, and in paintings. They appear in the forged iron grills of the doors and the windows. Other objects and tutelary images also protect the domestic premises. Portraits of Moses, Aaron, Maimonides, Rebbi Shem'un, Rebbi Meir and of the island's great rabbis stand next to a picture of President Bourguiba, and, at times even a photograph of Henry Kissinger, clipped out of a newspaper.

Courtyard of a house: on the left, the beams of the *succah*; on the right, the *succah* room, open to the sky, where meals are taken during the Festival of *Succoth*.

A Jerba interior: on the eastern wall, a square piece of fabric indicating the direction of Jerusalem and a *lulav* from the preceding *Succoth*. Here again, messianic expectation is etched into the very decoration of the house.

Entrance to a house decorated for a marriage. The candelabrum can be read as a palm tree with five branches or fish skeletons, which are prophylactic symbols.

A sacred space, traced by the wire of the *'eruv*.

The Shattered 'Eruv

For the last twenty years, this space, which combines the patterns of Arab-Muslim architecture with forms adapted to Jewish ritual and the Jewish calendar, has been undergoing profound changes. Some of these changes can be ascribed to the generally higher standard of living achieved by the country as a whole. Modern amenities have rendered traditional facilities obsolete. The ground-level hearth has yielded to the gas range. Running water has rendered the well unnecessary, while the refrigerator has taken over the well's function as a place of cold storage. The layout of the kitchen and the women's daily routines are also changing, and the stages and modalities of this revolution can be followed from house to house.

As the Jews have adopted architectural models which alter both their domestic space and their village's profile, many other changes have ensued. Not long ago, their houses lay under the shadow of the synagogues whose second story walls, pierced by twelve colored windows, dominated all the other buildings of the two Haras. For the last several years, economic success has been manifested by the construction of new houses and the radical modification of the old ones. The increasing height of these new structures proclaims their owner's economic ascent. In one case, a family erected a dome to crown its new mansion. People objected that the house looked like a mosque. Nonetheless, the height of houses, once uniform, has become a matter of competition. While the old style house was functional, the modifications which new tastes have imposed have made it necessary to abandon several of its original components. The mikveh has been replaced by a bathroom; the permanent room for Succoth has disappeared. And above all, space is being turned inside out. Formerly it was organized around an interior courtyard where women spent their secluded life. It is now turning outward, with the courtyard reduced to practically nothing, while the front of the house opens out onto peristyles, or huge terraces, or bulging windows. Open forms and closed spaces combine with each other in a fashion which is rather eccentric and not completely functional. Western models were borrowed before people knew how to use them, as in the case of "living rooms" where no one lives.

Like changes in dress, these innovations in surroundings can be seen in all of Tunisia. If they are able to control their diffusion and manifestation, the Jews are willing to accept them. However, they are not willing to accept changes imposed on them from the outside which call into question the life of the Jewish communities. The very names of their villages are now a subject of controversy. The local authorities banished the name of Hara Sghira and renamed it Riyad. The Hara, in Tunisian dialect, always signifies the Jewish quarter, whereas the name Riyad (meadow, garden) evokes serenity. In other words, the authorities want to stress that all forms of discrimination among Tunisians have disappeared and that there is no longer any need to perpetuate a ghetto. The Jews cling to the former name, as they cling to the distance and the history it implies. What was once perhaps an imprisonment is now claimed as a necessary condition of life.

Hara Kebira has been officially named As-Sawani, the gardens, which transforms it into a kind of suburb of Houmt Souk. The Jews ignore this name, and persist in thinking of the two Haras as Jewish territory. Waiting for one side or the other to impose its place name, the road signs have become illegible, and there is hardly any indication of the existence of a Jewish town. Names serve as vehicles for historical and political meanings and, in Jerba as elsewhere, toponymy is not a neutral subject.

In Dighet, even though the Muslim population is now in the majority, there is no mosque. Like the Ghriba, the mosque is located in the open countryside at some distance from the village. At certain hours of the day, one can hear two choruses simultaneously — the cantillation of the Jews from one side and childrens' voices reciting the Qur'an from the other. The Jews consider this mosque as a place of asylum. They claim that one day (perhaps during the revolt of 1864?) the Arabs rose up intending to attack the Jews. The Jews fled to

37

the mosque and locked themselves in. When their assailants caught up with them, they could not find the entrance, since the doors had miraculously become invisible. As for the Ghriba, while it is visited primarily by Jews, the Muslims also accord it a sacred character.

This arrangement illustrates the kind of tacit consensus which used to underlie relations between Jews and Muslims. In Hara Kebira, the consensus has fallen apart. In the haram space circumscribed by the two concentric cords of the 'eruv, the Jews have lived among themselves for several centuries. Nowadays the Muslims are more numerous, and this has altered the relationship which the Jews, above all the women, formerly had with this space. These new Muslim residents are immigrants from the mainland, who never had the experience of a structured interaction with the Jews. Relations between them are therefore unharmonious, anarchic and in need of redefinition.

In the last few years, another boundary has been crossed. A huge mosque has been built at the entrance to the village. Its minaret dominates the countryside, while the muezzin's voice — actually, a recording — fills the air of the Hara five times a day.

From time to time, the two cords of the 'eruv are cut or torn. The Jews are stubborn about setting it back in place, reinforcing it, and repairing the contours of the unbroken enclosure. The preservation of one's own space has become the stake in a daily war. People now regret the sale to the Muslims of houses left behind by emigrating Jews. They begin to dream: wouldn't the best solution be to build a new Hara, where others wouldn't be allowed to come?

Is this a nostalgia for the ghetto? Perhaps it means rather that the community has become aware that the loss of its territory to others deprives it of an essential condition of its life and its continuity.

---

1. The mezuzah is a piece of parchment inscribed with verses 4-9 of Deuteronomy VI and 13-21 of Deuteronomy XI, folded and attached to the doorpost of houses and rooms.

3
Communal Life
"Building a Wall around the Torah"

The Torah,
in its case
of painted wood.

A Theocratic Republic

Slightly more than 800 Jews live within the perimeter of the *'eruv* of Hara Kebira, and approximately 280 inhabit Hara Sghira. Their lives are geared toward the fulfilment of ritual. Work and leisure, the dietary and vestimentary rules, the system of private and institutional education, social relations, everything bears the imprint of religious law. Words, gestures and actions are always understood in terms of two central concepts: *haram*, forbidden / *halal*, permitted. Of Jewish thought and learning which developed outside of Jerba, it was primarily the legal literature which the Jerbans saw fit to appropriate. This, they supplemented with a systematic codification of their own customs. The norm for behavior is therefore explicit, taught to children, tirelessly recalled, and followed to the letter. It gave rise to a hyper-trophy of ritual which surrounds the slightest details of life. The Jerbans are like those people mentioned in the Talmud who, when they speak to God, say to him: "Lord of the universe, I have established more prescriptions than you have imposed on me, and I have respected all of them" (*'Eurbin,* 2lb). Stone by stone, they have built a mighty edifice which encompasses their entire lives.

Intimate knowledge of the Law and rigorous execution of its prescriptions seem to be the main preoccupation of these communities, and orthodoxy their dominant characteristic. Orthodoxy, it is true, is the monopoly of the male segment of the population. The men preserve, transmit, interpret, and, when necessary, bring the written tradition up to date. Only they know the sacred language of the Scriptures. During their decade-long careers at religious school, the *yeshiva*, young boys are introduced by stages to the Jerban learned culture. For women, a very different situation obtains. Until the recent opening of a girls' school they had no access to the texts. They shared the practical aspects of their religion with the men. They learned and related the *mirabilia* of the rabbis of Jerba. Their dreams could bring crucial messages. They knew and transmitted the oral culture in its local forms, but not the learned culture. In this, the communities of Jerba resemble many other Jewish communities, where the women's role is reduced to practicalities. They also bear a resem-blance to Muslim societies where literate and learned Islam has for a long time been the exclusive monopoly of men. The communities of Jerba have pushed this sex-division even further. Most notably, women in Jerba do not enter the synagogue. Only the Ghriba, which in every respect enjoys a special status, is open to them, as is the synagogue of Dightia in Hara Kebira, where they have access to a tiny cramped room. No space is reserved for them in any other place of worship. Women, crowded at the doors and windows of the synago-gues, are spectators from the religious ceremonies performed on the inside.

In Jewish law, the duty of prayer is incumbent only on men. Jerban rabbis have disap-proved of attempts to organize prayer services for women in the girls' school. Even though the girls are no longer illiterate, their religious instruction is practically oriented, excluding the Talmud and other advanced legal texts. Once out of school, they do not take part in the religious services nor in the study and compilation to which some of the men devote them-selves. It is hardly necessary to say that this clearly perceived asymmetry is unanimously accepted and legitimized. It is in the order of things, which everyone undertakes to preserve and reproduce. The changes which have taken place in the education of girls have not, until now, affected the traditional division of roles. It is as if everyone tacitly admitted that preservation of this division is essential to the survival of the community.

Officially, the two communities are subject to the Tunisian administrative system, whose recent expansion is plainly evident throughout the island. The local municipal authorities are responsible to a representative of the governor who has his seat in Houmt Souk, while the governor himself is in Gabes, some ninety miles away. Jerba is represented in the National Assembly. Since independence, the Tunisian state has set up or developed services of public welfare, education, security, transportation, tourism, and the like. The Jews of Jerba are the users and beneficiaries of this intricate system, but never active participants. Not a single Jerban Jew works in the government bureaucracy. They occupy no positions of authority at the local level nor, *a fortiori*, at the regional or national levels, even though from the legal point of view they are not denied access to such positions.

For them, what constitutes the *res publica* is what goes on inside their community, *po qahal qadosh Jerba*, "here, in the holy community of Jerba," as it is designated in their religious literature. There is no formal body which governs these communities. Up until the end of the Protectorate, rabbinical judges were officially appointed to deal with matters relating to personal status. Because of the nature of the communities, rabbinic authority extended to many aspects of social and economic life and reached its peak during the career of Rabbi Moshe Khalfon Hacohen, of whom we have already spoken. This scholar and religious judge served as Grand Rabbi of Hara Kebira from 1918 until 1950, and by the time of his death, had already entered the ranks of the miracle-working rabbis.

Since independence, Tunisian legislation is uniformly applicable to all Tunisian citizens, including, of course, the Jews. The government no longer appoints rabbinical judges, and the aspects of marriage, divorce and other matters of personal status are arranged within the community and have no official character. Up until the first years of independence, the Jews also had a *shaykh al-hara,* an intermediary between the communities and the local authorities. This function was never important, and people generally tried to avoid being appointed to it, especially since it entailed responsibility for assessing and collecting taxes, a task which put the shaykh in an uncomfortable position. The only other institution was the so-called *Comité,* founded in the colonial period to administer the communal funds derived from the proceeds of the tax on kosher meat and from the donations of the faithful on the occasion of the great festivals and the like.

Thus, what endowed the two communities with their vitality is not the strength of political institutions or of official administrative organs, but rather the participation of each individual in the life of the community, and the respect and reaffirmation of each individual for its collective norms. For this purpose, public opinion confers higher authority on a single rabbi and confides in him the responsibility for interpreting the law, for arbitrating conflicts, and for serving as a general guide to the community in matters both sacred and profane. His informal selection comes about because of his learning, his conduct, and his wisdom. Neither a diploma nor an investiture ceremony is needed. A rabbi is someone who behaves like a rabbi.

Once in this position, the rabbi expresses the *vox populi* much more than he changes it. He makes his pronouncements, most notably, in homilies and sermons, which he delivers orally in the Great Synagogue, one Saturday a month, and in pastoral letters whose text is distributed to all the synagogues and read to the congregation. These sermons, needless to say, are faithful to tradition. But this tradition is not a fixed body of prescriptions and prohibitions. It is kept alive by a permanent exchange between the community and its spokesman, with each conforming to the other. The rabbi's statement of position is awaited as a reassertion of the life of the community.

The chief rabbi also intervenes, in equally traditional fashion, by producing *responsa* every time a relatively unusual problem arises. For instance, a young mother who had experienced several miscarriages, gave birth to a male child. According to Jewish law, if the first fruit of the womb is a male child, it must be given to God and can be reappropriated by the parents only after the *fidyun* — the child's redemption from a *kohen*, a ceremony which occurs thirty days after his birth. Was the newborn infant, in this case, to be considered as the first fruit of his mother's womb and was a fidyun ceremony required? It was on this question that the rabbi of Jerba was called upon to pronounce. This was not a novel problem; it had been confronted before. And, in the vast literature of Jewish law it had been discussed, elucidated and decided by the most distinguished rabbinic authorities. A single reference to one of the numerous precedents would have been sufficient to settle the matter. Instead, the rabbi produced a lengthy written response (approximately 26 handwritten pages) thereby reaffirming publicly that in this community of Jerba, the law, its interpretation and application are alive, well and relevant.

Another example illustrating how local tradition is constantly coming to the fore relates to the dietary laws. For a fixed annual sum, a certain family in Hara Kebira had bought the exclusive right to purchase the edible organs (heart, liver, tongue, etc.) of slaughtered animals. As she was preparing a meal, a woman of this family found a needle embedded in the liver of one of these animals, which immediately rendered all the meat unfit for consumption. She dropped everything and brought the question before the rabbi. As the verdict was awaited, all culinary activity in the village ceased. The old timers, who had experienced similar situations in the past, made predictions on possible outcomes. The rabbi took great pains and considerable time to gather the necessary material. Finally, he produced a *responsum* based on a local precedent: only the defiled portion of the animal was forbidden, the rest was declared kosher.

As we can see, the rabbi has a consultative role. When he prescribes the norm, general opinion is taken into account together with jurisprudence and local usage. This general opinion changes with time. In the recent past, the rabbis were able to outlaw the phonograph. How could Jews rejoice before the Temple is rebuilt? How could they accept the mixing of men and women in music and dancing? But today, no rabbi has attempted to prohibit the use of cassettes, which has become widespread.

When a rabbi proposes rules which are considered too harsh, someone may take the risk of violating them. This is a grave matter; deviations from the norm are frowned upon, because they not only involve those who commit them, but also risk misfortune for the entire community. Moreover, the rabbi has at his disposal a number of public sanctions. The most feared measure is for him to declare the offender's wine non-kosher. A young Jerban who had played cards, spent time at the beachfront hotels, dared to meet with his fiancé before their wedding, and persisted in his wrongdoing in spite of the rabbi's repeated warnings, was condemned in this way. All dealings with him were suspended. Before he could marry, he had to present himself in front of the rabbi, barefoot and with his face covered by a burnous, in order to have the ban against him lifted.

In this theocratic republic, performance of the various religious tasks is distributed widely among the members of the community. Certain families assume responsibility for the upkeep of the synagogues. One jeweler, who also serves as schoolmaster, sees to the slaughtering of poultry and every Friday afternoon heralds the arrival of the Sabbath by sounding the *shofar* from the rooftops. Another inspects the wires which constitute the 'eruv to make sure that they are unbroken.

The *mohel* who circumcises the newborn males is also a jeweler. In the synagogue, all the men participate in the prayer service, and any one of them is capable of serving as prayer leader. Above all, everyone is prepared from infancy for this continuous, supportive participation in the life of the community.

There are also informal groupings which fulfill diverse communal functions. When a person dies, the corpse is prepared and wrapped in a shroud by a brotherhood of volunteers. When a girl from a poor family is about to get married, yet another voluntary association provides her with financial assistance and takes responsibility for collecting funds for her wedding and trousseau. Other groups are in charge of visiting the sick. There is an organization for educational advancement, "The Light of the Torah Society," which has been functioning since the beginning of the century. In the days when scorpions claimed several victims every summer, a brigade of young people was formed to hunt them down. These organizations have no legal existence. Participation in them is spontaneous, and they are managed without any bureaucratic apparatus whatsoever. In one way or another, they make everyone responsible for the smooth running of things.

Every matter is therefore subject to a spontaneous orchestration and everybody takes part in the concert of activities. The only way to escape it is to leave the island. Since every-

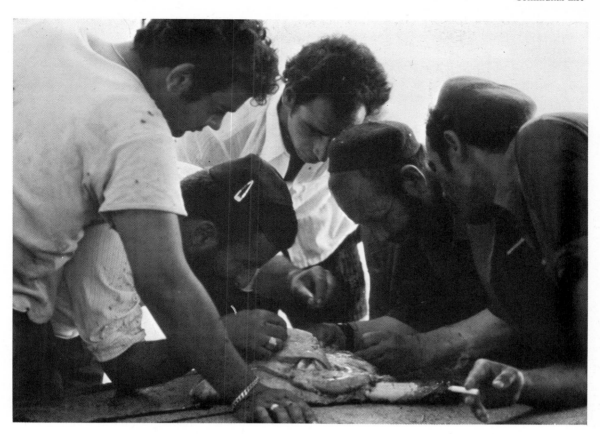

Above:
inspection to
determine whether
the slaughtered animal
is kosher or not.
Left:
inside a synagogue,
a locked collection box
for charitable donations.

one who remains belongs to an ethnic group, anyone who stopped conforming to its norms would be condemned to remain outside the social fabric, suspended without rights, without a network and without speech. Consequently, ascription to a group becomes prescriptive. As seen from within and as seen from without, belonging to a group means being in it from birth until death.

Growing Up
in a Jerban Family

The primary units which make up the social fabric are the households designated in Jerba by the Arabic term *dar*. As in the rest of Tunisia, dar means both the family which bears a single name, and the building which shelters them. It brings several generations, or several young couples, together under one roof. Married sons live with their fathers, or else settle in a house which is connected to their father's. Consequently, it is nearly impossible to count the exact number of independent units. For all of Hara Kebira, their number exceeds 120. The largest single household includes 20 people, consisting of the head of the family, his wife, his mother, their 13 living children and a nephew and a niece whose mother had died (figures 6 and 7). The niece had just married, but contrary to custom, the bridegroom owned no house. He therefore joined this large family, bringing his aged mother with him. It will probably not be too long before the young wife, in her turn, will give birth to a child.

In another household, the father and mother had 18 children between 1943 and 1966; of these 16 survived. Eight of them are now married. Only one of the daughters has left Jerba. All the other daughters are still there, and the eldest began to have children when the mother bore her fourteenth living child. As for the married sons, two of them live with their parents, and the eldest is already the father of six children. Another son lives with his wife and three children in an adjacent dwelling, connected by a passageway to the paternal house.

There are, on the other hand, families like that of Rabbi Sion, which have been reduced to practically nothing. His wife and children have emigrated to Israel, but he refuses to follow them. Nourished alternately by different families in the Hara, he lives alone with his guard dogs, but will not tear himself away from Jerba.

There are, on the average, six or seven persons per household. The households consisting of ten or more persons (twenty- eight in all), add up to 341 persons, or 42.4% of the Jewish population of Hara Kebira. In Dighet, the population of 280 inhabitants is divided into 31 households, an average of nine people per household.

If emigration were not reducing the size of families, the Hara would now be in an optimal position for reproduction and development. Infant mortality and childbirth deaths have been reduced to practically zero. Women continue to reproduce during the entire period of their fertility. The age of mothers at the birth of their last child is known in 67 cases. The most frequent is 39 years (14 times); but 20 women had children at a later age, that is, in 29.5% of the cases, while the most senior of them all was still giving birth at the age of 47. Eleven women had periods of fertility of 20 years and more, giving birth to a total of 104 living children (an average of 9.4 per mother). The largest number start to bring children into the world when they are between the ages of 20 and 30. But 23 of the 89 women whose age at the time of the birth of their first child is known, that is, one woman out of four, began earlier: one of them at the age of 14, three others at 15.

At this pace, it is possible today to have fine, large families. Thirty years ago, this happened but rarely. Death carried children off at birth, or in their first years. Out of 100 children who were born before summer, we are told, fewer than twenty survived to the autumn. Mothers did not know how to take care of children. They were kept confined to the house, they were rarely bathed and poverty and undernourishment were prevalent. Indeed, the testimony of the Jerbans is confirmed by archives. Of 106 children born in 1946, only 33 were still alive in 1948; of 37 children born during the first six months of 1947, 15 were dead in 1948. The richest families were not much better protected than any others. Sixteen children were born to the richest Jewish family on the island in the 20's and 30's; of these only three daughters survived to adulthood. And even then, one died at the age of 19, and another at 34, carried off by typhoid.

In 1948-49, a Jewish doctor — the Jerbans would not have allowed non-Jews to examine

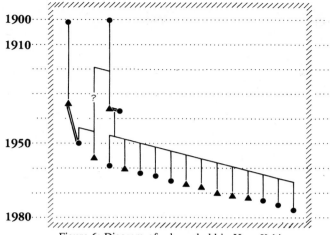

Figure 6: Diagram of a household in Hara Kebira.

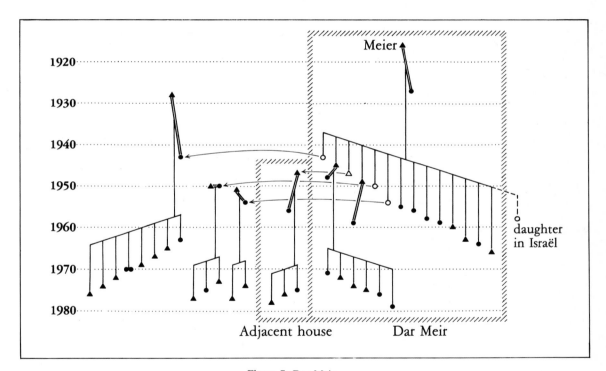

Figure 7: Dar Meir.

them — and his team described the situation in the Jewish settlements of southern Tunisia and the battle which had been undertaken to introduce new rules of hygiene and nutrition:

It sometimes happens that women have as many as twenty pregnancies to keep one or two children or ... none at all. Furthermore, the prevailing ignorance of even the most elementary principles of hygiene leads one to suppose that, were it not for the sun and the perfect climate, there would not be a single Jew in Jerba today.

Recently, one of our nurses found, as she was making her rounds, a baby which was severely bloated. She insisted that it should be brought to the doctor. But there was a grandmother around; it's useless to consult a doctor when somebody knows how to take care of everything, as she does. In this case,

45

the following was the treatment: cover the little body in a thick layer of clay and wrap it tightly in bandages from head to toe. The result was not long in coming. The baby died.[1]

It is common knowledge that marriages between blood relations result in offspring whose state of health is often precarious. Such marriages are almost the rule, especially in Al-Hamma and in Jerba.

Miscarriages are considered a normal phenomenon. A woman can easily have 7 or 8 miscarriages, but she won't consider it unusual, because her mother, her sister, her neighbor have had just as many.

An infant, upon birth, is relegated to the corner of the house which is farthest from the front door, and for six months, it is denied the right to see the light of day. It is not allowed to enjoy any of the healthy effects of the rays of the sun, nor to breathe a little pure air.

Children who are breastfed are nourished only in this way until they are two years old or even older, and their mothers are surprised when they find that their children are still unable to stand up straight.[2]

Even though the rules of hygiene and nutrition introduced by Tunisian doctors have now become firmly rooted, death and sickness are still not viewed as strictly natural calamities. If they strike this child or that family, it is a sure sign that malign influences have been at work: al-'ayn. Until recently, mothers deployed all the weapons of magic against the evil eye: talismans hung over children's beds and on their clothing, apotropaic first names, disguising of boys with girls' names and clothing, and so on. Today, certain types of talisman have been given up. But Jerbans still make their children wear jewels in the shape of amulets. They still guard the door of a woman in labor by posting on it a text which shows a picture of a hand and a fish. They insist that after she has given birth, the mother should not wash, so as to avoid envy. Finally, they give their children, especially the boys, names borrowed from the world of the sea: Bougide (mullet), Qarus (bass), Sbirsa, Uzifa (sardine), Huita (little fish), Bahri (the fisherman).

Nowadays, these names have been demoted to a second or third position, and mothers entrust their children's health, as well as their own, to the doctor. Death, together with the fear it inspired, has retreated somewhat. At the very moment when the chances for reproduction were reaching their highest point, birth control made its appearance. Despite majority opinion, and the rabbi's disapproval, several couples in Hara Kebira have adopted some form of family-planning. This Malthusian trend has apparently not yet reached Hara Sghira.

As in the rest of North Africa, the birth of a girl is not welcomed. Nonetheless, in some places people do celebrate the birth and naming of a girl, the piercing of her ears a few years later, and finally, her reaching menarche. None of this happens in Jerba, where the only female rite of passage (though a splendid one) is that of marriage. When a boy is born, there is a circumcision and, if he is the first-born, there is the ceremony of the *fidyun* in which, a month later, the newborn son is symbolically redeemed from the *kohen* by his parents. Unlike other North African communities, the Jerbans celebrate the *bar mitzva* (the moment at which the boy puts on the *tefilin* and becomes an adult in legal and religious matters) without much fuss. In any case, this episode changes nothing in his life since the rabbinic curriculum is usually completed a year or two after the bar mitzva. The boy then enters adult life.

Marriage

Every man is obliged to take a wife so as to increase and multiply. And he who does not fulfill this obligation is like one who sheds blood and diminishes the human race, and he causes the separation of the *Shekhina* (the Divine Presence) from the community.

A book published in Jerba by a young rabbi, Messiad Madar, on the subject of family ethics, *The Gates of Purity* (*Sha'arei Tahara*, Jerba, 1963) forcefully invokes this commandment of the *Shulkhan 'Arukh* and bolsters the argument of the text by citing the fact that in his day, the Grand Rabbi of Jerba, Moshe Khalfon Hacohen, appointed a special rabbi to deal exclusively with family matters in the community. The ideal thus, is to get married so as to produce the largest possible number of children, and then to marry them off while they are young and with strict attention to their descending order, with boys and girls treated as two independent series. If for any reason one of the children is late in getting married, his or her younger siblings are delayed accordingly.

For Jerban Jewish girls, to marry young means to do so around the age of 18. A generation ago, marriage at the age of menarche or even before, was still practiced. One girl, who married at the age of 14 in 1944, was unable to become a mother for four years. Another married at the age of 11, and became a mother one year later. She was only twelve years older than her first-born son. She had seven of them, without counting her daughters; each son was named after a prophet. When the first daughter got married, the mother was still fertile, and nursed both her own son and her grandson at the same time. Another woman, today in Israel, married at the age of 9, had only one daughter, and then went mad and was unable to take care of her child. The daughter was brought up in the families of relatives and although steeped in piety, she still has not found a husband. The Jerbans ascribe all these misfortunes to a marriage which, it is now decided, was too early.

In Tunisia, marriage is not permitted before the age of 18. Among the Jews of Jerba, of 123 marriages performed between 1962 and 1977, the age of the bride ranged from 14 to 59. There is no case of marriage before the age of 14 and it is rare for a girl to marry after the age of 33. The greatest frequency is between 16 and 25. The average age is 21.

The men's ages are between 18 and 69; the greatest frequency is between 19 and 34, and the average is 27. It is rare for a bridegroom to be over 40.

Marriages performed between 1962 and 1977 (123 cases)		
	Women	Men
Minimum age	14	18
Maximum age	59	69
Average age	21	27
Greatest frequency	16-25	19-34

One observes a discrepancy in age at the time of marriage of men and women, and a shorter span of optimal years for the girls. The time of greatest frequency is spread out over 15 years for the men, and only over 9 years for the women. Whereas for men, late marriages can come after the age of 38, for women over the age of 27 it is a rare occurrence. And what is more, a man can remarry, whereas a widow or a divorced woman has practically no chance of finding a second husband.

Marriages of girls around the age of menarche have entirely disappeared. Only three marriages of girls under the age of 16 were performed since 1962. A period of waiting therefore separates puberty from marriage, a tendency which can be observed in the rest of Tunisian society as well.

Usually, the husband is older than the wife. However, in seven cases there was no difference in age, and in 21 cases the wife was older than the husband, the difference in age rarely exceeding two years. The men were older in 94 cases, and the difference in age ranged from 1 to 23 years.

A woman, therefore, is generally considered to be marriageable until she is 27, while there is no age limit for a man. Needless to say, these patterns are not "natural," since a woman between the age of 27 and menopause can still produce numerous progeny — something which is not unusual in Jerba. But the optimal age is still placed quite low, and families are anxious to marry off their daughters from that moment on. The girls of Dighet keep close track of the sex ratio in their village. If they include young children in their count, the number of girls and boys is equal. But when they calculate only the young people of marriageable age, the ratio is unfavorable for girls, and measures must be taken either to export some of them, or to write some of them off. This is a terrible situation, which runs the risk of preventing younger sisters from getting married.

All the same, families are not prepared to give away their daughters to just anyone. A man is expected to behave according to the rules of the community, and to be a diligent, eager worker. People do not seem to worry about physical qualities. Thirty years ago, it is said, piety was placed above everything else. A father preferred to have his daughters marry rabbis, even if this meant having to contribute to their upkeep. This assertion, which is impossible to verify, speaks of a nostalgia — or a desire — for a time when religious values prevailed uncontested. Nowadays, affluence and ability to get by in life come before piety. Being ready for marriage requires that a man display his wealth. When he buys a car, or builds a house or an apartment and equips it with modern conveniences, he is announcing that he is a good match.

Girls are supposed to be young, pretty, well-behaved and from a good family. Pretty means with white skin, light eyes and smooth, abundant hair. Those girls who are cursed with a dark complexion are in continual torment, cleaving to the walls to avoid exposure to the heat of the sun. Even in the middle of summer, they wear heavy stockings to protect their legs from the sun. One canon of beauty is changing, that concerning the female silhouette. A thin woman is still considered sickly in Hara Sghira; in Hara Kebira, however, people have already switched to western models, and slender shapes are definitely triumphing over the more ample figures of the recent past. In both villages, young girls are no longer fattened in the weeks which precede their wedding. But in Dighet, they are fed enough to round out their figures. They are sheltered from the light to make them pale, and at the same time to protect them from the evil eye. In both villages, one of the preparations for a wedding consists of covering the arms and legs of the bride-to-be with a thick layer of leavened dough, which has the effect of making her skin lighter.

Propriety and a good education are part of the family capital of which the young woman is the bearer. These qualities are manifested by her modesty, her quiet demeanor, her knowledge of all household skills, and her docility. She may speak freely, but she may not speak maliciously or stridently. A family's good reputation, and brothers of good character are considered a sufficient guarantee for the young lady's good behavior and her ability to manage a household.

Marriages seem to be contracted according to these few conditions. There is no visible hierarchy among the families, due perhaps to the reduced size of the two communities. The only discernible tendency is towards marriage between literate families. One can guess at the inferior status of some families which are *déclassé* or stricken by misfortune (sickness, the misdeeds of some of their members), and at the superior status of those families which are thought to be very old. However, these positions are fragile, and each generation can and must work at maintaining or changing them. In any case, all marriages take place within the Jewish population. Not a single example of intermarriage with Muslims is known. During the colonial period, a few Jews did marry Christians, but their descendants have left Jerba. Among the Jews, local endogamy is very strong. Jerba does exchange spouses with its own archipelago — Medenine, Tatahouine, Zarzis, Ben Gardane — and sometimes, with its emigrant colonies in Tunis, Marseilles, Paris or Israel. Hara Sghira gives wives to Hara Kebira. But for the most part, marriages are concluded within each village.

Like the other Tunisian communities, the Jews of Jerba shared certain customs with their Muslim neighbors. The first of these is endogamy: not only marriage with one's paternal cousin, (the *bint 'amm* characteristic of Arab marriage customs), but also marriages

48

between uncles and nieces, between maternal cousins, and double combinations (a brother and a sister contracting a marriage at the same time with a brother and a sister from another family). Among the families now living in Hara Kebira, there are seventeen cases of marriages between close relations. While this is a large proportion of the total number, the Jerbans maintain that in the old days, such alliances were more common. The second feature which North African Jews shared with the Muslims was polygamy. This was forbidden in Tunisia in 1958. Apparently, it was rare among the Jews of Jerba. But people preserve the memory of a rabbi at the beginning of this century, whose four wives exhausted themselves in domestic battles, and of the man who took his wife's sister as his second bride, since the first one had not succeeded in giving him any children.

In the West, families usually go through a cycle of several distinct and temporally extended stages: from the formation of the couple to the time of the birth of the first child, then the period of childbearing during which the family expands, followed by a contracting of the family, through the scattering of the new generation, or the death of the parents. The birth of the youngest child and that of the first grandchild are separated by an interval and also by distance, since the new household establishes itself on its own.

In Jerba, this cycle is never intentionally interrupted. Only sickness and death can break it. And since, when children marry, they settle in their father's house, even if they have to enlarge it with new construction, the size of the families should actually vary little, with births making up for deaths. But in fact, emigration has seriously diminished the size of many families.

Women's Space

No one is ever alone in a Jerban House. Shuishna told us: "All week long, you don't go out, you don't see anyone, all you do is work at home. But on Saturday, you have visitors, you meet people, you go out." In fact, during the week, people get together all the time. First of all, there is the school, where young children and teenage girls pursue their studies and where others come for simple distraction. The schoolteachers, like the cooks in the school canteens, are local girls. The school is open. A very young child, or an idle housewife can go into the school at any time, sit down in the classroom and knit, sew or gossip, while the class goes on. If someone gets there at mealtime, then he or she stays on to share the meal with his or her children. There is no stiffness or formality, and since the school is located in a former private house, everyone feels at home there.

Young girls spend the afternoon together with other girls their own age, now at one house, now at another. They knit, crochet, sew or make talismans to the accompaniment of the radio or the television. They stop whatever they are doing to follow television serials. Through these programs, the girls acquire a familiarity with the fine points of Egyptian and Lebanese Arabic much greater than that possessed by their elders and their brothers, thus participating unconsciously in the broad movement of Arabization currently speading all over North Africa.

Girls cluster in small groups, sharing their knowledge and skills, teaching one another the techniques of knitting and embroidery. And since everything here takes on a ritual aspect, when a new embroidery pattern has been perfected, it is a fair certainty that it will be reproduced in every house. One summer, the reigning fashion was sheepdogs embroidered in cross-stitch on canvas and stretched on frames of white wood. The following year, beds, bicycle seats, benches, were all covered with wool crocheted in the same pattern and the same colors.

Young girls are constantly on the move from one house to another. They come to borrow a household item, to draw water from the cistern, to bring a cooked dish from one household to another, or to carry some item of news or gossip which will mobilize the women of the other households.

On Saturday, games replace chores and television. The girls squat in the courtyard on the ground and play with dice, with dominos, or with glass pearls. They break up into small groups to walk around the village. In Hara Sghira they avoid the alleys where the boys gather, which frequently causes them to go far out of their way. They all meet again at *Dar Zohra*, Zohra's house, with other girls, small children, and young mothers surrounded by their offspring. Zohra is a poor madwoman, the last descendant of a family which was once very well off and which left her the house in which she lives. The families of Dighet converted this house into a kind of asylum for the three paupers of the village: Zohra, a feeble-minded man, and Baba Gagou from Gabes. A putrid smell pervades the premises, but this does not deter the girls. They bring food to the three unfortunates, spoonfeed the madwoman, change her diapers and clean the house. There are 20 to 25 of them in the courtyard, and they talk about the latest television serial, of the joys and sorrows of a famous actor, or of local life. Every evening, the same scenario is repeated, as the girls go to Dar Zohra to bring food and to exchange news. The old man from Gabes, who is almost blind, sings a tune in Arabic, and the young girls respond with a refrain. Nightfall sends everyone home and brings back the quiet.

Hara Kebira does not have a poorhouse nor any other locale comparable to Dar Zohra. Its young girls, almost invisible during the rest of the week, gather on Saturdays at their school or, in defiance of endless rabbinic warnings, take their stroll on the streets of the village. A "courtship parade" takes up part of the afternoon. Eligible girls show off their luxuriant hair and appear in new outfits and high heels. Boys and girls do not exchange a single word and, supposedly, not even a glance. But the two groups are aware of one another, and marriages are silently arranged in this merry-go-round manner.

The women have other meeting-places. Even though they do not take part in the synagogue prayers, they are charged with the care of the Ghriba and of some synagogues in Hara Kebira. On Thursdays, in preparation for the Sabbath, they gather at the synagogue in little groups. They clean the oil lamps, change and light the candles, shake out the mats, and sweep the rooms. While they are performing these duties, the men may not enter the synagogue.

The other meeting-place which is reserved for the women is the *mikveh*, where married women purify themselves after their monthly periods. One family is entrusted with the key to the bath and sees to it that the *tbila* takes place according to the norms. Women come and go very discretely, trying to escape the gaze of strangers. Nevertheless, they are noticed. When a woman comes to the bath, other women know that after her visit, she will be having sexual relations with her husband, and they exchange knowing glances. When her visits to the mikveh cease, it is because she is pregnant. The village women keep an accurate account and can forecast with precision when the child can be expected.

They also exchange visits. In Hara Sghira, a young bride, absorbed in establishing her husband's household, still longs for her own family. She may, therefore, if her in-laws consent, and after she has completed all of her domestic tasks, escape for a brief visit to her mother and sisters. In Hara Kebira, this grave question is covered by a rabbinic ruling which authorizes women to visit their father's house on Mondays, Thursdays and Saturdays.

Saturday is the visiting-day par excellence. Women favor the houses in which some important event has taken place, such as sickness, a birth, the arrival of news from the outside concerning a member of the family who has emigrated, an engagement, or a death. News is known immediately, since a member of the family concerned becomes the door-to-door messenger as soon as something has happened. It would be an insult to a household not to inform it of some important episode. It is also an insult not to respond in the proper manner, that is, with a visit and with words and gestures appropriate to the circumstances. If a death occurs, the women keep the mourners company throughout the entire week following the

Women at the Ghriba: the opportunities of meeting are frequent, but women rarely expose themselves
to the public view and the separation of sexes is rigorously observed.

death. Hara Sghira still has its professional mourners, specialists in eulogizing the dead and
in uttering the ululation of grief. These have disappeared in Hara Kebira, but its women still
hold their week-long vigils. Similarly, a wedding requires eight days of gatherings.

In any case, it is within the space circumscribed by the two cords of the 'eruv that the
young girls and the women move around. They do not cross the market square, and they do
not leave the village. In fact, before the opening of the girls' school put an end to their
seclusion, their lives were usually divided between two houses: first their father's, and then
their husband's. Marriage is the move from one to the other, and the bride makes this transition behind layers of veils, without seeing or being seen. There are women in Hara Kebira
who hardly know any neighborhood other than the ones in which they grew up and into
which they were married.

Male Sociability

For the men, it is a completely different matter. All public, organized activities require their
participation. They have at their disposal several spaces which they enter by stages. As small
boys, they live in the house, i.e. in the women's quarters. Once they have reached the age of
four, they divide their time between the yeshiva — an exclusively male world — and the
home. They begin to spend time in the synagogue, and, as they get older, in the other male

gathering places: the market place, the craftsmen's shops, the street, and around a public cistern at which many of the men come together at dusk. On Friday afternoon, when they are free from school, young boys descend as a horde on the market of Houmt Souk, now deserted by the Muslims who are either at the mosque or at home, resting. With adolescence, they enter the work cycle, but generally still remain in the Hara for some years. The last barrier is crossed when a craftsman sets himself up in the market of Houmt Souk. By now, he has traversed the three spaces of house, synagogue and market.

Not everyone is willing to complete this itinerary. One can sense a kind of contradiction between piety and religious contemplation on the one hand, and the habits of the market-place on the other. The most learned and the most pious are rarely seen in the *suq*, and never in the coffeehouse, which other men frequent in the evenings to mix with Muslims and to play dominos. A fervently pious man tells us that he did not know the suq until the age of 35. He was already married and the father of grown children, but continued to devote himself entirely to study. His father's death tore him away from his texts and forced him into the marketplace. Once again, the space of the market seems to be the place of mingling, of communication which can lead to corruption.

Shared Festivals, Separate Spaces

In the Hara, no event is experienced alone. This is as true for individuals as it is for families. Everyone takes part and everyone has a stake in what takes place. Anyone who evades participation places the equilibrium of society in question and the community in danger. By doing so, not only does one express thoughts or intentions which are highly suspicious with respect to the family or group concerned, but one also runs the risk of causing widespread misfortune. Important events, while experienced collectively, are the occasion for separate ceremonies in which the distribution of roles according to sex is strictly observed, whether it be celebration of a wedding, mourning a death, or preparation for a circumcision.

In the case of a circumcision, female and male ceremonies take place one after another. On the day before the event, married women accompanied by their little children gather in the late afternoon. Young girls take no part in the celebration. In the center of the court-yard, one woman presides over the proceedings. Throughout the ceremony, gestures directly associated with the impending circumcision mingle with rituals of female fertility. The tools for the ceremony: a copper mortar, a knife, a pair of tweezers, a *kanoun* — a terracotta brazier — and a pair of scissors. Sitting on the ground, the leader begins by pounding sweet-smelling plants in the mortar. She then passes it on to the other women, who form a circle and pound the mortar each in turn. Every time one of them begins to pound the mortar, the *zgharit* (ululations) explode. Next, the leader cuts a piece of bright orange-yellow cloth for the garment the newborn child will wear during the circumcision. Each woman shares in sewing the different parts of the costume. Meanwhile, eggs are being hardboiled on the kanoun and are distributed to be consumed together with boiled beans flavored with cumin and salt. In the kanoun, the leader burns incense and gum, which she picks up with the tip of a knife and mixes in the mortar. She makes pellets out of the mixture, applies them to the baby's clothing and sticks dry beans on them, five per garment. Two women, standing shoulder to shoulder, murmur ritual songs in which the name of the prophet Elijah recurs frequently. The women fill small bags with sweet-smelling herbs and ground incense. Eggs, beans, beer and drinks are continuously passed around, and the ground is quickly covered with bean parings and broken eggshells.

Next, the tiny garment is dipped into a container into which water from the cistern and a fistful of sweet-smelling herbs have been poured. Each woman dips her hand into this brew, moistens her face with it; some also dampen their armpits or their abdomen, uttering noisy sighs of relief. A pot containing small bags of incense and herbs, a jug of water, hard-boiled eggs and cooked beans are then brought to the mother, who has remained invisible throughout the ceremony. She drinks a glass of the water in which the child's garment was dipped. This garment is hung up in the room to dry. After this, the women leave. Everything on the floor is swept up. The women's gathering is over; night falls.

Now it is the turn of the men. They gather in the same courtyard for the *leylat az-zohar*, the night of the Zohar. They read together, sing *piyyutim* which call for the arrival of the Messiah, and eat and drink far into the night. The father of the newborn boy reads a special passage from the Zohar. It is only in the early morning, at the very moment of the circumcision that men and women converge on the same place. Even then, they are still separated spatially: the women huddle together in the room where the mother is reclining, the entrance to which is hidden by silk hangings, while the men stand outside in the courtyard. Between the two groups, at the entrance to the room, and exposed to the light is the chair of the prophet Elijah upon which the operation is going to take place. The father, the rabbis and the mohel stay in this frontier zone. After the child has been circumcised and has received his names, and after the mohel has exhibited his fingers spotted with blood in all directions, the women furtively eat hardboiled eggs and beans, and leave. The men then seat themselves at tables in the courtyard and, together with the children, eat, drink, pray and sing for several more hours.

Much more could be said about the symbolism of these gestures and of the food which is consumed and distributed in each of these encounters. Even more could be said about their religious significance. But what we wish to emphasize here is the social character of every individual happening and the fact that "private" happenings simply do not exist. No invitation is required to take part in the circumcision cermony. It is open to all members of the community. The privilege of picking up the foreskin in a clay pot, of showing the tools of the operation to the assembled men, and of marking the threshold of the room with blood from the foreskin, is sold twice a year at the great synagogue. It is a *mitzva*, which benefits the person who acquires it; the proceeds go to the community's charitable works. Thus, the birth of a boy in a family has a community dimension. Moreover, every rite of passage anticipates the future of the persons involved and announces what is to come afterward. This future depends on the quality of the ceremony which, in its turn, is a function of the conduct of the entire group. If everyone performs the movements and pronounces the expected words with precision and in the prescribed time, then the consequences will be satisfactory for all.

Peril from Within:
the 'Inara

This permanent orchestration of events is intended to preserve or to attain a harmony which is always endangered. The threat does not emanate from non-Jews. Muslims can use overt violence; they can mistreat you, despise you, even envy you. They will cause you harm, but they will not bring you misfortune. The *'inara* (evil eye) can come only from within the community, from Jews themselves. It manifests itself through the rapid recurrence of misfortunes within one household. People struggle valiantly to foresee the danger, to ward off its blows, to identify and to disarm the adversary.

A certain family in the Hara was doing rather well. After humble beginnings, the father had attained a comfortable affluence and had raised a large family including several grown sons. He volunteered to travel to Beja to buy wheat which the community needed for Passover and he took his nineteen-year-old son along on this trip. A truck accident killed the sone and injured the father. A terrible story; but one bows before fate. This boy had been

E

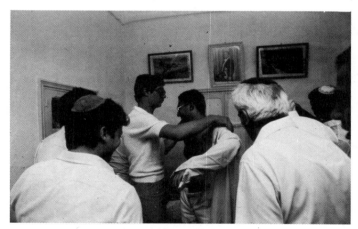

A marriage in Hara Kebira:
the village musician
(*left page*);
the veiled bride being led
to the house of her future husband
(*above*).
The bridegroom being
dressed by his friends,
led to the synagogue
and then accompanied
back to his home (*left*).

In Hara Sghira,
celebration after
a circumcision.

living in Marseilles. What made him come back? Why did his father drag him along on this trip? Clearly, God had counted him among the dead for that year. He had an appointment with death.

But one week later, another son, recently married, barely escaped a car accident while driving with his wife. This time, it was too much. "There's something there, and something has to be done." "There's something there:" this is the diagnosis of friends and relatives, who won't say more, but who do not fail to alert the family. "Something has to be done:" the threat must be deflected, cut short, by a mitzva, a good act.

The Jews wage a constant preventive war against the 'inara by filling their lives with the protective symbols to which we have already alluded (first names, talismans, pictures, etc.). They avoid ostentation and speak softly to avoid attracting attention. In their interaction with other Jews, they exercise constant vigilance. One has to show good will while indicating no suspicion of evil intentions on the part of one's interlocutor. One weighs one's words carefully, avoiding those which might elicit mistrust. For five you say: "Count your hand," for fifty, "half of a hundred," for fish, "the one from the sea," or "on the enemy's face." You take the precaution of excusing yourself before you pronounce ambiguous words, which might cause harm: *hashek, hashe oujhek, hashe 'ainek.* The art of speaking is part of the art of keeping peace or of waging war.

If misfortune strikes, then a defensive war is opened on two fronts. The first objective is to disarm the adversary. To identify him, but to do nothing to aggravate matters any further, and to avoid an offensive strategy. A counterattack would run the risk of increasing the difficulties. People are therefore content with carefully observing and containing the supposed aggressor. At the same time, they must enlist God on their side through a good deed. In general, it is enough to distribute a meal to the poor or to the readers of the Ghriba, and to have prayers said on one's behalf. But there is a hierarchy of mitzvot. In a certain household of Dighet where misfortune had struck multiple blows — one child stricken by a grave illness, two accidental deaths, a marriage-contract broken off, a divorce — the eldest son of the family had a synagogue built alongside the house and had a new Torah scroll written at his own expense. This was a long and costly undertaking. A full year was required to prepare the parchment, to write the entire text without the slightest mistake, and to check it over again and again. Supporting the scribe, Rebbi Haim, for a year while he did this work was in itself a great mitzva, all the more spectacular in that nothing like it had been seen for a long time in either of the two Haras. It was also a mitzva because the son, as it happened, was carrying out his late father's wish. His father, who died in an accident, had for a long time hoped to have a new Torah scroll written. But there is more: some envious neighbors, in an inexplicable outburst of temper, had said: "May no stone of that house remain standing." Therefore, they built a house for God within the house itself. Three times a week, for an entire year, the men were required to come to pray there, and on Thursday, the women had to clean it. In this way, they would make the house invulnerable, and all their neighbors responsible with them for its preservation.

When the synagogue was dedicated, and then again after the Torah had remained there for a year, the family prepared a colossal meal, not only for the poor and the readers of the Ghriba, but for the entire village and even for the people of Hara Kebira.

According to rule, the new Torah was carried to the Ghriba after a year had elapsed. The synagogue was reappropriated by the household for domestic purposes. The eldest son, recently married, transformed its space into his bedroom. Who would still dare to threaten it? He had measured up to adversity and had found an answer to the great misfortunes which his household had undergone.

Separation of Genres

In all the social manifestations we have already described, one principle remains constant: the separation of genres. Mixing, *khalta*, is distasteful to the Jews of Jerba. As is known, the principle of the homogeneity of classes and of species occupies an important place in Jewish tradition. Just as one does not harness a donkey and an ox to the same yoke, just as one does not weave linen and wool together in the same cloth, so one does not, in the social order, allow men and women to mix together. When the question arose of whether or not to provide lunches to schoolboys and schoolgirls in the same place — not at the same time — the rabbi of Hara Kebira forbade this because of his opposition to *ta'rovet*, the mixing of species.

A fortiori, mixing with the Muslims is not tolerated. Not that the Jews live in complete isolation. In fact, they are in constant contact with the population of the island. Jerban society is more than a background canvas, it is a condition of life for the two communities. But however basic the interaction between Jews and Muslims may be, it takes place within borders which are clearly delineated, and according to rules which are no less rigorous for being tacitly understood. There are certain areas where interaction is simply impossible. Since, among the Jews, every moment of life is powerfully ritualized, entire stretches of lived experience cannot be shared. We shall mention these later on.

In sexual matters, the taboo is absolute. Exchanging women is unthinkable. In other words, Jews and Muslims cannot be relatives, and cannot treat one another as such. In North Africa, it is the language of kinship which organizes all representations of the social world, and all social relations are, in turn, seen to be structured as a function of these representations. Consequently, we can imagine the extent of the barrier which this reciprocal taboo raises.

Exchanges of food are asymmetrical. In a general way, the same foodstuffs are forbidden to both groups and, since animals are slaughtered according to similar methods, nothing prevents Muslims from eating the food of the Jews. Jews, however, can eat only kosher meat, slaughtered under rabbinic supervision. Since their meat is not kosher, any food cooked in Muslim utensils in a Muslim kitchen cannot be eaten by Jews. A Muslim and a Jew can be the closest of friends, friends unto death, as the local expression has it, but they cannot share a table except for drinks and raw food. Muslim friends who own plots or gardens bring presents of fruit, grains or dates after every harvest, but always in their natural state. Quite probably, this preoccupation with dietary purity plays a large role in maintaining domestic self-sufficiency. Almost everything which is eaten has been prepared in the house.

There are people who carry this preoccupation so far as to soak glasses or cups for several days, if a non-Jew has drunk from them, or to stop using a cistern, if non-Jews have drawn water from it. A certain rabbi instructed the members of his own family not to accept food even from other Jewish families. These, admittedly, are extreme cases. Indeed, among the Jews we can measure the quality of social relations by the quantity of prepared dishes exchanged. Cooking seals a marriage alliance and a friendship, and symbolizes hospitality. Conversely, to tell a Jew that his wine is impure is tantamount to expelling him from the community, and is one of the sanctions which the rabbi imposes on wayward Jews. We should recall the parallel descriptions of Maimonides and al-Idrisi. In Jerba, the obsession with purity common to Jews and Ibadis inclines both groups towards mutual exclusion.

From Community to Minority

To preserve their identity, Jerban Jews have put in place a protective system of exclusion and enclosure. They erected a series of barriers around their communities, and every time one of these crumbles, another is raised in its place. "Build a fence around the Torah" (*Talmud, Pirkei Avot*). By following this injunction to the letter, the Jerbans have maintained their cultural integrity. But it is by no means sure that they will long be able to sustain this policy with the same success. For this fortress is mainly defensive, and the only weapons in its arsenal are symbolic.

Fighting the evil eye: antidote
for headaches in the form of a bird's head,
a clove of garlic suspended from the ceiling...

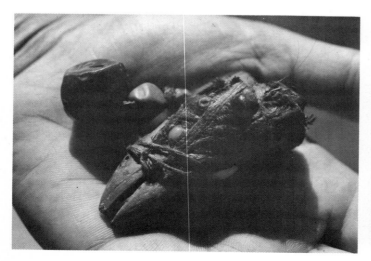

Once you have passed beyond the circle of people whom you know, you reach a world where indifference and neutrality are *not* the rules of the game. The fact that everyone is assigned to his own group implies that people from different groups do not ignore each other, even when they do not know each other. The small incidents of daily life, the gibes, the dirty tricks, the occasional openly hostile actions, regularly remind the Jews that though they are tolerated, they live under the domination of others. While the status of the *dhimmi* has disappeared, the corresponding condition still exits. The Jews who are most deeply anchored in tradition have a word to define it, *galut*, the exile in which the Jewish people live, and from which they can expect nothing but misery and slavery until the day of redemption. Meanwhile, the only strategy is resignation. A Jerban author explains this phenomenon.

> The Jew was always subject to humiliations, to wrath, to false accusations. But he was used to it, and accepted the full implications of galut, of life in exile. He bent his head under every storm which came to disturb his peaceful life. . . . He bore this burden with joy as long as his neighbors accorded him minimal rights; in exchange for these he gave up the right to walk among them with his head held high.[3]

Since independence, the conditions of this *modus vivendi* have changed. Only recently, both Jews and Muslims were without any power. Like the rest of the country, Jerban society was divided up into collective entities, more or less walled off from one another by language (Berber or Arabic), by religious affiliation (Ibadism, Maliki or Hanafi Sunnism) or simply by ties of kinship. Beyond these, the state seemed remote and inaccessible. Now, even though local differences are still maintained and visible, all Muslims take part in a national system with a state and its representatives. They can participate in the political system and benefit from it on the local level. But the Tunisian state, while preaching an ideology of equality and unity, is neither secular nor pluralist. Therefore, the Jews — who themselves are strangers to any secularist ideology — are, de facto, excluded from the politi-

... a string of fish tails protecting the entrance of a house, a hand holding a string of fishes, wall painting around the doors of a house where a marriage is celebrated.

cal game and placed in the position of being dominated by the majority group. They are changing from a community into a minority. When the need arises, they respond to collective threats through traditional means — penitence and recourse to patronage. While the rabbi decrees prayer and fasting within the community, others, on the outside, bring into play the relations of clientage which unite the Jews to various influential people in the area and, by stages, to influential people in the capital. Collective memory has kept alive the precedent of the Jerban family which gave asylum to Jews during the revolt of 1864. One century later, the descendants of this family are expected to fulfill the same role.

Paradoxically, young Jerban Jews no longer speak about galut. Like other Tunisians, they have been brought up with the political language of an independent Tunisia, and have internalized one of its major themes: condemnation of *isti'mar,* of colonialism and domination. The young people do not accept their state of subjection. They have appropriated this nationalist discourse, but have no way of applying it to their own situation within Tunisia. Hence this oscillation between two imperfect choices, between turning inward and turning outward, between withdrawal back into the confines of the Hara or of emigration from it. Withdrawal within its confines would maintain an active civic life within the narrow horizons of the community and would allow the community to endure; emigration would shatter this collective life whose preservation they are striving to safeguard.

In 1926, the population of the two communities was 3,800, in 1936, 4,100, in 1946 over 4,300. If they had developed at the same demographic pace as the rest of Tunisia, the Jews of Jerba would now number 15,000. The establishment of the state of Israel in 1948, the independence of Tunisia in 1956, the forced creation of cooperatives which severely upset local economic life in the early 1960's, then the Arab-Israeli wars of 1967 and 1973 were each followed by waves of emigration — mostly to Israel. Consequently the Jewish population fell to 2,600 by 1956, 1,900 by 1967 and to 1,200 at the present time. The Jerban communities are amputated and their ability to reproduce themselves as a collective unit is in serious question. Outside Jerba, however, it might not be possible at all.

1.   B. PEREZ, in *OSE Tunisie*, Bulletin Trimestriel, no. 1, January-March, 1948.
2.   *Op. cit.*, No. 7, July-September 1949.
3.   Boaz HADDAD, *Jerba Yehudit*, Jerusalem, 1978.

4
The Rhythm of Time
Being Jewish,
A Full Time Activity

Blessed art Thou, O Lord our God,
King of the Universe, who divides the holy from the profane,
Light from darkness, Israel from the nations,
The seventh day from the six other days of work.
Blessed art Thou, O Lord, who divides the holy from the profane.

The Havdalah (distinction) prayer,
recited at the conclusion of the Sabbath.

The synagogue, house of God, house of men.

Time as a Parameter of Identity

Time, like other cultural elements, traces a line which separates Muslims from Jews. Each group has its own calendar, its own names for the months and its own count for the years. In the year 1401 of Islam, the Jews were in 5741 (1981-82). Since the colonial period, the Christian calendar and system of dating have been added to the two others and continue to regulate administrative and civic celebrations. While retaining a knowledge of its neighbor's important moments, each group lives according to its own calendar.

From the Islamic calendar, the Jews are familiar with the five prayers which punctuate the day, the solemn observance of Friday and the great festivals of the annual cycle. They feel uneasy about the month of pilgrimage since, so they say, people come back from it with less tolerance for the Jews than they had when they left. During the month of Ramadan, they observe the slowing down of life during the day, its intensity at night and the increased consumption of food. In symmetrical fashion, the Muslims recognize the important moments of the Jewish cycle: the Sabbath, when the Jews close their shops, dress differently and do not smoke; and the great festivals, which the Muslims name according to the meals associated with them. *'Id et-tmar,* the festival of fruit, is the New Year because of its association with the consumption of fruit and new dates; *'Id ed-djaj,* the festival of poultry, is Yom Kippur; *'Id el-ftira,* the festival of unleavened bread, designates Passover, and *'Id el-qli,* the festival of roasted seeds, designates *Shavu'oth.*

Each group recognizes only the outward ritual manifestations of the other's practices without really understanding their underlying meaning. They note whatever has a bearing on communications between Jews and non-Jews, since exchanges between them have to be adapted to these two rhythms of time. The Muslim calendar is strictly lunar whereas that of the Jews is luni-solar. The Muslim year has 12 months, each consisting of either 28 or 29 days, so that the sequence of months does not correspond to the rhythm of the seasons. The Jewish years has twelve months consisting of 29 or 30 days, and every two or three years a thirteenth month readjusts the lunar to the solar cycle, and consequently, to the agrarian cycle. Festivals, therefore, recur every year at the same season.

While the two groups divided the year differently, the week, the days and their lesser subdivisions are held in common and are designated by the same names. However, these measurements, identical in quantity, do not have the same properties, the same qualities. The prohibitions, prescriptions and practices which are attached to every moment are not the same; in a word, the social uses of time vary according to which group one belongs to.

The Muslims, like the Jews, divide the day into two parts: the first is the night, the second, the day. The Jews greet the beginning of the day at the synagogue, with the *ma'ariv* evening prayers after which they return home for the night. The night is filled with a religious atmosphere. A blessing precedes and follows the family meal. Before they go to bed, the men recite the *shema'* — the profession of faith, and the final prayer which accompanies a man at his death. When the believer wakes up, he renders thanks to God, with the prayer *modeh ani,* for having given him back his life, for its is believed that the soul of a sleeping man returns to the Eternal One. During the night, dreams are the medium through which God sends His messages, with the family's dead, or well-known deceased rabbis who consistently appear in white clothing, acting as intermediaries. These are instructions which must be obeyed. Night is therefore the moment in which communication with the Invisible can take place. Night ends just as it began, in the synagogue, where the men gather for the *shaharit* prayer.

Following the shaharit prayer, each person sets out on his daily tasks. This is the time when secular activities and interaction with non-Jews take place. In the middle of the day, the men return home to have their meal, without any detours to the synagogue. This non-break is a recent custom, made possible by the motorbike and the automobile. Before these means of transportation were introduced, no one went home for the mid-day meal. Either

Participation in the rituals is universal and recognizes no hierarchy.
Here, a mechanic leads the morning services.

you brought it with you from home, or else a messenger gathered all the lunches from the households of the Hara and brought them to the market of Houmt Souk. You could also have lunch at one of the inexpensive kosher eating-houses at Houmt Souk which have now disappeared. In any case, lunch is still a less important and less copious meal than dinner. It is eaten quickly, and does not involve a gathering of the entire family.

At the end of the day, after work, the men once again converge on the synagogue, where the *minha* (late afternoon) prayer is linked to the ma'ariv of the following day. The men's lives and itineraries are therefore regularly balanced between two opposite directions: from the synagogue to the home at night, the time and place of the sacred; and from the synagogue to the market during the day, the time and place of the secular (figure 8).

Within the week, there is the same opposition between ordinary days and festive days. In years gone by, when many Jews worked "in the *ghaba*," that is, outside of the two Haras, they were absent from Sunday until Thursday, but returned and spent the rest of the week in the Hara. Secular activities and secular space were therefore clearly separated from the time spent in the sacred space. Within the home itself, this opposition is expressed by a choreography in three movements: random, from Sunday until Wednesday; feverish and noisy, on Thursday and Friday; and slow and silent on the Sabbath. Beginning on Thursday, shopping is done for the Sabbath and the synagogues are cleaned. On Friday, people rush about to clean the house, to cook, to bathe, to finish all the preparations on time. They cross the courtyard a hundred times in every direction, and kiss the *mezuzot* on the thresholds that many times. Before sundown, the dead are honored. In the houses and synagogues, candles are lit for the community's dead, for the great rabbis, and for

64

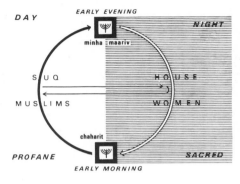

Figure 8: Daily itinerary.

Torah reading during a weekday.

In the synagogue, conversation at dusk between the *minha* and *ma'ariv* services.

Friday afternoon fever: every family
carries its Sabbath meal to the communal oven.

the deceased members of one's own family. At last, the women rest at the threshold of their houses, while the men congregate around a public cistern near the entrance to the Hara and await the sound of the *shofar*. From a rooftop, the shofar is sounded first to call for the suspension of all activity; and then again, ten minutes later, to announce that the Sabbath is about to begin.

After a service in the synagogue, the men exchange greetings of *shabbat shalom*, "Sabbath of peace," and go home. Calm and quiet settle on the streets of the two villages. In the houses, celebrations are beginning. As in all observant Jewish households the world over, the linen and the dishes have a special sparkle on this evening. The bread made by the mother of the family has an unaccustomed flavor; the blessings over the wine, the bread and the herbs have a special seriousness. *Kabud shabbat*, the honor of the Sabbath, requires abundance. The couscous, the main dish of the evening meal, laden with several kinds of meat, is richer than the one prepared for weekdays. The main dish of the meal which follows the prayer of Saturday morning is the *tfina arisha*, wheat cooked overnight in the communal oven with meat or fish and garnished with eggs hardened in the oven. Invariably, all the Jewish families of Jerba prepare and eat identical dishes on the Sabbath. When they are able to, they send a sack of wheat to their absent relatives so that they too can enjoy a similar ritual meal with the same ingredients in Paris, Marseilles or Tel Aviv.

Sabbath is the day for ostentation, for preening and for displaying one's best clothing. Friday night is the recommended time for conjugal union, and the women prepare themselves by putting on their best clothes, and by covering themselves with perfumes and jewels.

Saturday is the day of prayer and meditation, when the men spend several hours in and around the synagogues. In the early morning, each of them, wrapped in his prayer shawl, goes to his preferred synagogue. There is no order or hierarchy in the use of space. In each synagogue, one of the congregants — and not necessarily the same one every week — leads the service. After the profession of faith, they pronounce the silent benedictions facing in the direction of Jerusalem. The prayer leader repeats the benedictions out loud, while the congregation proclaims as a chorus, "Blessed be He, blessed be His name." This recitation is followed by the most solemn moment of the services: the removal of the scrolls of the Torah from the ark. Members of the congregation vie for the privilege of carrying the Torah scrolls from the ark. It is one of several *mitzvot* which are sold to the highest bidder at an

66

"Remember the Sabbath day, to keep it holy. Six days you shall labor, and do all your work;
but the seventh day is a Sabbath to the Lord your God, on it you shall not do any work." (Exodus 20:8-11)

A trayful of breads baked in the communal oven for the Sabbath;
each loaf bears the family's distinctive mark.

"auction" during the services. The congregation passes before the holy ark in procession.
The ark is opened and the scrolls are removed and paraded around the synagogue before
being set down on the *bimah*, the raised platform in the center of the synagogue. After the
weekly portion is read, the ceremony culminiates when the Torah scroll is lifted above the
heads of the congregation which shouts in chorus: "Here is the Torah which God set before
Moses and the people of Israel."

Before returning the scrolls to the ark, the weekly epistle of the chief rabbi is read to the
congregants. The conclusion of the Torah ceremony is followed by a *musaf*, or additional
service — a brief prayer service reserved for Sabbaths and major festivals after which the con-

gregation disperse to their homes to bless the bread and wine and to take the Saturday meal.

This ceremony which — except for the reading of the rabbi's proclamations and of the "additional" service — is repeated in shortened form on Mondays and Thursday, is common

Every week, on the eve of the Sabbath, and every month, on the eve of the new moon, women light candles in the memory of the dead.

to all Jewry. Jerba stands out here only because of the participation of every adult male of the community. They gather once again in the afternoon to read, study, or at least to chat in the shade of the synagogues until the minha prayer. After the ma'ariv, the Sabbath ends just as it began, with exchanges of greetings, *shavu'a tov*, a good week.

Saturday is the day of *lemma*, of gatherings in houses, in the streets, in the synagogues. A sadness suffuses the heart when, once the blessing for the end of Sabbath has been pronounced, a week of lonely work and of worldly activities begins.

All of this seems to be regulated in a very uniform fashion. Doesn't it become boring to repeat the same actions over and over? Not at all. Everyone, knowing the score by heart, takes pleasure in performing according to his talent or his virtuosity, and is happy simply to excel in that which is required by custom. Not innovation, but perfection in applying the norm is the prized quality. Observing the Sabbath to its last detail remains, together with adherence to the dietary laws and those prohibiting intermarriage, one of the three major prescriptions which no Jerban Jew would transgress.

Like the day and the week, the year also contains alternating high and low points in the intensity of ritual activity. The year is marked by two great cycles of three weeks each. One begins with the Jewish New Year in the autumn, and the other with the spring. At these times, absent members of the family return to the ancestral home and, from the initial preparations for the festival until their concluding ceremonies, the full energies of the household are mobilized.

The Calendar for the Year 5739

From the annual cycle to the single day, the observance of time is for Jews one of the means of ascription to their own group and of demarcation from those who order their lives according to another rhythm. On the subject of the dates of new moons, or of the festivals and of all the gestures which they involve, Jerban Jews are infallible. Nonetheless, a printed guide of the year's events is published annually on a single large sheet of paper and is posted

Figure 9: The calendar of the year 5739.

in every synagogue. We reproduce here the calendar for the year 5739 (1978-79) (figure 9).

This calendar begins by showing the symbolic value of the year, obtained by changing its numbers into letters, and then finding an appropriate Biblical verse which announces what the year promises. "Yes, says 5739, I will send you the prophet Elijah."

The text informs us that this is a regular year, numbering twelve months and fifty Saturdays — fifty Sabbaths — on which all the activities which we have described will be repeated. Then comes the list of the twelve Jewish months of the year, from *Tishri* through *Elul*, with the dates of the major festivals as well as the minor holidays. Another section of the calendar gives the dates of the new moons. What does that involve? For the men, a special prayer; for the women, lighting candles and taking a day's vacation from their normal work. There is another section, which has a different series of divisions of the year: the *tekufot*, the beginning of which marks the transition from one season to the next. This is a critical period, as moments of passage always are, entailing the rotation of the angels who stand guard over the water. During this changing of the guard, death threatens anyone who consumes water. Jerban Jews empty out all vessels containing water and, according to a custom known to other North African communities in times past, they refrain from drinking during the several hours taken up by the changing of the guard.

All of these tables are in Hebrew. There is only one passage in Judeo-Arabic, giving "the seasons of the year according to the Gentiles"; that is, the solar calendar, with its four seasons, its twelve months, and the days on which the various agricultural operations take place. Even after the advent of Islam, the Julian calendar, which regulated agricultural activity, remained in use all over North Africa together with the Muslim lunar calendar. The next two sections of the calendar give the corresponding dates for the Jewish, Christian and Muslim calendars; that is, for "Israel, Edom and Ishmael."

The last section of the document deals with practical magic, enumerating the days on which it is dangerous to take blood, to write charms and the days when one should avoid pronouncing vows, and so on.

The calendar combines the historical and religious time of the Jews with solar and agricultural time, with Muslim time, and with Christian time; for all of these divisions have an impact on Jewish social life.

The Annual Cycle

To describe the annual cycle of Jerban celebrations, the particular modalities of those practices which they share with Judaism the world over, the countless local customs which evoke usages familiar to all North African Jews or which are particular only to Jerba, would be an endless task.

Their time is a full time. It is saturated with events and has several stories to tell: a natural, cosmic story, with the two cycles of autumn and spring, and the four tekufot or seasons which we have already mentioned. There is also the midwinter fast, the tenth of *Tevet*, the fast of 17 *Tammuz* in July, and the December pilgrimage during which people light bonfires while the moon delays its appearance. It is also a story of nature tamed, of edible plants, of useful animals and of living beings, with corresponding sacrifices and alimentary rituals. Finally, there is also the time of sacred history which recalls and recounts the joys and sorrows of the Jews from Creation until the destruction of the Temple. These three levels of time are superimposed on one another, and historical commemorations cover cosmic and agricultural rituals. The same process of temporal sedimentation certainly occurs among Jews in other parts of the world. But in Jerba the different levels are clearly visible and give rise to a corresponding display of gestures and actions.

Time is full. At the conclusion of one celebration, people have already begun to prepare for the next one. Festivals echo one another. Even the periods which seem to be empty have particular connotations. *Heshvan*, the second month of the year which follows the great autumn cycle, is not marked by any celebration — with the exception of the introduction into the silent devotion of the prayer for rain, the timing of which Jerba shares only with Palestine. Heshvan is a bitter month in which no marriages are celebrated. After Hanukka and the December pilgrimage to Al-Hamma, near Gabes, there are ten weeks which are only mildly interrupted by the festival of trees in February. This entire period is marked by confinement and seclusion. *Fi ibit makla u rqad al-bit*, in the month of Tevet, the proverb says, you can only eat and sleep at home. *Shbat isabbat u-ikhobbot u-iluah al-'azuz fiz-znaq*, the month of *Shevat* shakes and knocks down and throws old ladies into the streets. This stretch of dreary time has its parallel in the weeks of mourning which follow the festive period of spring.

Time is full. The rituals required by each celebration mobilize all the members of the community and, through prayer, oblations, consumption of food, the care devoted to the body and to the home, impinge on life and death, on individual fortunes and collective destiny.

Several groups of protagonists are active in the scenario in which these rituals are accomplished: men, women, young boys, and young girls. Each has its well-defined role. Men excel in the liturgy, although they are active in other realms as well. Women, on the other hand, occupy a preeminent, though not exclusive, position in the practical rituals, especially those relating to food. On Fridays and each new moon, they also oversee the cult of the dead. As in other aspects of culture, the female presence is all the more forceful when the rituals refer to the most archaic and least spiritualized layers of religion. Young boys take the initiative in rituals of social inversion and in ritual games at Purim, Passover, during the month of *Av*, and in inaugurating periods of renewal and prophylactic actions. Young girls, as far as we know, have a specific role on only two occasions, which we shall describe, and which prepares them for serving as repositories for the community's practical memory.

At two crucial moments of the year another unexpected group, the non-Jews, enters upon this grand ritual scenario. It is they who furnish the markets with the specific products required for the celebration of the spring and autumn festivals.

From the Autumn to the Spring Cycle

The Jewish year begins with the autumn celebrations which last for three weeks and the period is framed by the festivals of *Rosh ha-Shanah* and *Succoth*. More than a month before Rosh ha-Shana, one already senses a holiday atmosphere in the community. The 20th day of the month of Av — forty days before the New Year — inaugurates a series of four encounters in which men release one another from engagements undertaken, but not fulfilled, in the course of the preceding year. On the 20th day of Av, the congregation divides into two groups. The first group is seated and acts as a tribunal; the second stands and asks to be released from its unfulfilled obligations. The two groups then exchange their roles. They repeat the same ceremony on the first evening of the month of Elul, or 40 days before Yom Kippur, and then again on the eve of the New Year. The entire series reaches its culmination with the solemn *kol nidre* prayer on Yom Kippur eve. The Saturday before Rosh ha-Shanah is also one of the four special Sabbaths of the year on which the rabbi solemnly pronounces a *drash* — homily — to the entire community, which is then followed by a collection of funds for the benefit of the association charged with the care of the sick.

Rosh ha-Shanah is a festival which partakes both of agricultural time and of purely religious time. It is the moment when God suspends the fate of each member of the community and of every element of nature. Themes of judgment and repentance appear in all the practices associated with this great cycle. In the days before Rosh ha-Shanah, the children go to the fields to pick the first olives of the season; on the eve of the New Year, they run through the streets of the Hara, proclaiming "Here are the olives of *yehi-rason*, may His will be done." On the eve of the festival, the service at the synagogue is followed by a ritual meal, designated by some people as a *seder*, which brings together all the members of the family. All of its elements are laden with symbolic value. Not only do the Jerbans gather all the first fruits of the season — first olives, first dates, first pomegranates — but, in addition, they play with words, making use of the analogies of color and flavor, of homonyms and homophones, to usher in a clear, sweet and fertile year. On the festive table, salt is replaced by sugar. People eat squash, leeks, garlic, a lamb's head and its broiled heart and lungs. For every dish, the formula "May His will be done" is repeated. On the second night[1], cooked beans dipped in honey, dates, pomegranates and jam form part of the meal. Why so many dishes? The Jerbans explain: We choose sweet dishes and we season them with sugar so that the year will be sweet; we eat a lamb's head so that the Jews will occupy the most prominent place. We eat the lungs so that the year will be light, and the heart to open our hearts to the Torah. We eat pomegranate so that our virtues may be as numerous as its seeds. The Arabic word for beans evokes the Hebrew root for growth; squash and leeks, respectively *kra'* and *kerat* in Arabic, refer to the verbs "tear" and "destroy" in Hebrew, and so, to the destruction of our sins.

On New Year's Day, the Jews do not take a siesta — God might count them as dead — and, instead, gather at the synagogue. At the end of the afternoon service, they share a watermelon, the last one of the season. To bring it to the synagogue, to offer it to the congregation is considered a privilege. The meaning of this custom, which appears to be peculiar to Jerba, is not clear. According to local exegesis, it fulfills the formula: "If your sins were like scarlet thread, they shall be white as snow." Thus, the Jerban Jews symbolically consume their sins. Whatever its significance, this practice does not detain them from proceeding to the ceremony of the *tashlich* which is common to all the Jews of the world. At the end of the day, they go as a group to a well or to the sea to drown their sins in water.

Here, as in other places, society renews itself on the occasion of the great festivals. In Jerba, these festivals allow the community to reaffirm its existence. Prayers on the High Holy Days take place in only four of Hara Kebira's eleven synagogues, and only in the Ghriba for Hara Sghira. Without exception, the entire male population is in attendance and fully participating. On these occasions, the sale of various privileges related to worship generate considerable revenues destined for community-wide purposes and not, as is the case during the rest of the year, simply for the local synagogues. The auctions of various ritual privileges during these holidays provide the largest part of the community's budget for education and charitable works. All the men are present at the great synagogue to hear the rabbi's sermon on the Saturday which falls between the New Year and Yom Kippur.

Rosh ha-Shanah inaugurates a period of intensive religious activity, of penance and of a cessation of profane pursuits. As for Jews everywhere, the day after Rosh ha-Shanah is a fast day, but one which in Jerba is observed quite strictly. Preparations for Yom Kippur, the day of atonement, of affliction and of purification, begin immediately. As for other Jews, Yom Kippur consists, first of all, of a sacrifice of substitution and of expiation. Three days before, each *shohet* (ritual slaughterer) in the community submits his blades for the inspection of his colleagues, to verify that they are in a perfect state. On the ninth of Tishri, the day immediately preceding Yom Kippur, the head of the family takes a fowl for each member of the family — male for a boy, female for a girl — and twirls it over their heads three times. These birds are then sacrificed, to be eaten after Yom Kippur. In the afternoon, preceding the fast, married men carry lamps to the synagogue, one for each male in the family. An effort is made to keep the lamp lit continuously until the next festival, Succoth, during which oil lamps burn consecutively for eight days in the *succah*, the holday booth. Before the sounding of the shofar which solemnly inaugurates the fast of Yom Kippur, men and women take a ritual bath. The women send the meal which will be eaten after the fast to the public oven. The men assemble in the courtyard of the synagogue to receive thirty-nine strokes with a whip, a ceremony symbolizing the expiation of their sins.

With penance and prayer the fast then begins. Then men are dressed in white and go barefoot; they pray in the synagogue until a very late hour, and again the next day from the early morning until the end of the afternoon. Of all the customs which root Judaism so firmly in Jerban soil, one of the most remarkable is the supplement which the Jerbans have introduced into the kol nidre prayer which opens the Yom Kippur service. This added prayer is simply a list containing, in chronological order, the names of the great rabbis and

To the left:
Celebration of *Succoth*
in a synagogue of Hara Kebira.
Below:
Simhat Torah, the joy of the Torah.
Celebration at the conclusion
of the annual cycle of Torah readings.
With the reading of Genesis,
the new cycle commences immediately.

scholars of the Jewish tradition and concluding with a full enumeration of Jerba's own major rabbis from the eighteenth century to the present. Thus, at the most solemn religious moment of the year, this additional prayer explicitly establishes a continuity between the great spiritual masters of the past and their own local learned men and themselves.

On Yom Kippur afternoon, children join their fathers in the synagogue, where, covered by prayer shawls, they receive their blessing. With nightfall, the shofar anounces the end of the fast. The married men bring the oil lamps home with them and after breaking the fast, they return the oil lamps to the synagogue.

> On the fifteenth day of the seventh month, when you have gathered in the produce of the land, you shall keep the feast of the Lord seven days; on the first day shall be a solemn rest. And you shall take on the first day the fruit of goodly trees, branches of palm trees, and boughs of leafy trees and willows of the brook; and you shall rejoice before the Lord your God seven days. You shall keep it as a feast to the Lord seven days in the year; it is a statute forever throughout your generations; you shall keep it in the seventh month. You shall dwell in booths for seven days; all that are native in Israel shall dwell in booths, that your generations may know that I made the people of Israel dwell in booths when I brought them out of the land of Egypt. I am the Lord your God.
> Thus Moses declared to the people of Israel the appointed feasts of the Lord.
>
> (Leviticus, XXIII, 39-43)

This passage from Leviticus, while outlining the prescriptions of the festival of Succoth also clearly points to its double meaning. On the one hand, it is an agricultural festival, an occasion for rejoicing at the completion of the harvest; on the other hand, a historical festival commemorating the exodus from Egypt. The text says in the seventh month because in remote antiquity, the New Year began in the spring on the first day of *Nisan*. We have

73

already referred briefly to the decoration of booths for this festival. The oil lamps of Yom Kippur are hung on walls decorated with silk fabrics. Fresh fruit, grapes, pomegranates, dates, lemons, peppers, eggplants, branches of myrtle and dried fish are suspended from the palm branches of the ceiling. The prophet Elijah's seat occupies its own place against one of the walls. The symbol of the alliance between God and His people is therefore added to agricultural symbols of fertility and renewal, as the symbol of messianic expectation of redemption is added to that of a new exodus from captivity.

On the fifteenth of Tishri, *lulavim* are sold in the synagogues. They consist of a willow branch, a myrtle branch, and a palm frond, all tied together. They are held in the right hand, while the left hand holds an *etrog* (citron). During the seven days of the festival, the Jews recite the *hallel*[2] every morning as they turn toward the East, with the lulav in their right hand, and the etrog in their left hand. Once every morning, and seven times on the last day, the congregation walks around the bimah — the raised platform in the center of the synagogue. For this is the last day in the process of judgment which began three weeks earlier with Rosh ha-Shanah.

Two days later comes *Simhat Torah*. When the last part of Deuteronomy has been read, the congregation returns immediately to the story of the creation of the world with the reading of the book of Genesis. Amidst great joy, the scrolls of the Torah are carried around seven times. The cosmic, agricultural and religious cycles end and begin at the same time, while in the religious schools new subjects and texts are also being started.

The festival of Passover, occurring exactly six months later, is symmetrical to this autumn cycle. This relationship between the spring and autumn festivals is made tangible by the fruits of the Succah, which are preserved and eaten at Passover and by the lamb, bought at Passover to be fattened and sacrificed at Rosh ha-Shanah. There is, therefore, a connecting thread between the two major ritual cycles of the year.

Two important holidays — *Hanukka* and *Purim* — punctuate the interval between Succoth and Passover. The first, on the 25th day of *Kislev*, commemorates a historical event and its accompanying miracles. In the second century before our era, the Jews, under the command of Simon the Hasmonean, resisted the decree of Antiochus which imposed the worship of the Greek gods on the Jewish population of Palestine. In 165 B.C.E., they reconsecrated the Temple which Antiochus had pillaged and desecrated, and later established an independent kingdom in Judea and other parts of Palestine. According to legend, when they came to reconsecrate the profaned Temple by rekindling the eternal lamp, the Hasmoneans found only enough ritually pure oil for one day. Yet this oil burned for eight days. In Jerba, as elsewhere, people begin with one candle and light an additional candle each evening until, by the eighth night, the entire candelabrum is illuminated. This ritual of fire and light probably goes back to a more ancient cult, linked to the natural cycle and to the winter solstice, as does the festival of *Lag Ba'omer*. which falls in the month of May and which will be described below. Both holidays are occasions for pilgrimage.

During the festival of Hanukka, at the new moon of Tevet, the *Hillula* of Sidi Youssef al-Ma'rabi takes place. Hillula means wedding, but must be understood here as "death," and consequently, the mystic marriage of the pious man. On the Sunday closest to the first day of Tevet the Jews of Jerba go to Al-Hamma of Gabes to pay homage at Sidi Youssef's tomb. According to legend, he was a disciple of Rab Ari — that is to say, Isaac Luria, the famous sixteenth century cabalist who lived in Safed. When the Master gave the order for his disciples to disperse, Sidi Youssef travelled as far West as Al-Hamma. As he was approaching death one Friday afternoon, he requested to be buried before the Sabbath. The sun stood still in its course long enough for this holy man's last wish to be respected.

With the winter solstice and the death of Sidi Youssef, time is suspended; with the reconsecration of the Temple commemorated by Hanukka, light reappears. All of these elements overlap at Al-Hamma where the pilgrims kindle large bonfires next to the tomb of Sidi Youssef al-Ma'rabi.

74

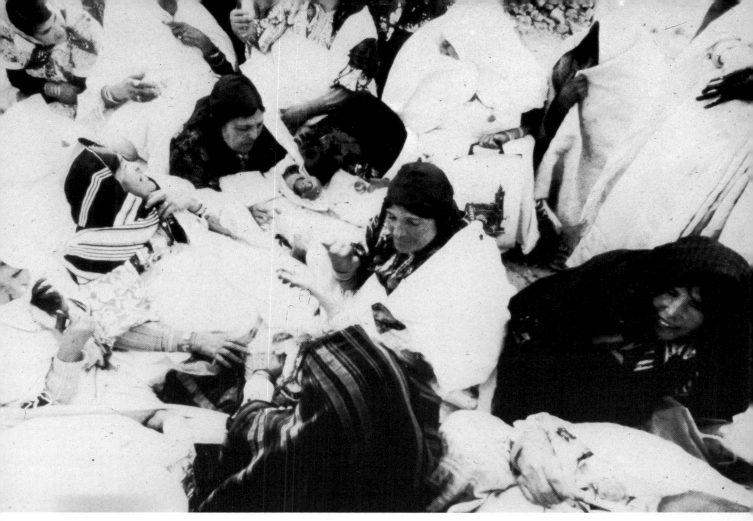

A local cult: the pilgrimage to the tomb of Sidi Youssef al-Ma'rabi at Al-Hamma near Gabes, celebrates his "mystic union" with God, and corresponds to the winter solstice.

After this solar festival, Tevet and Shevat are cold, dark months. On the tenth of Tevet, a public fast marks the middle of winter. On its fifteenth day, the month of Shevat is punctuated by a minor holiday, the New Year of the Trees. In its honor, Jerban Jews prepare a special dish called *bsisa*, a mixture of grains, lentils, oil and sugar to which they add grapes and dates. Since the trees leave their places to visit each other during the night, it is recommended that people stay home on that evening.

From Spring to Autumn

Then comes *Adar*, special because of the celebration of Purim. Purim is presented as a historical festival which recalls how Esther, wife of the Persian king Ahasuerus, rescued the Jews from the death and destruction which Haman, evil counselor of the King, had determined for them. It is an apocryphal story. But Jews have preserved it as an allegory of victory over their enemies.

Now in the twelfth month, which is the month of Adar, on the thirteenth day of the same, when the King's command and edict were about to be executed, on the very day when the enemies of the Jews hoped to get the mastery over them, but which had been changed to a day when the Jews should get the mastery over their foes, the Jews gathered in their cities throughout all the provinces of King Ahasuerus to lay hands on such as sought their hurt. And no one could make a stand against them, for the fear of them had fallen upon all peoples. All the princes of the provinces and the satraps and

75

the governors and the royal officials also helped the Jews, for the fear of Mordecai had fallen upon them.

(Esther, IX:1-3)

And Mordecai recorded these things, and sent letters to all Jews who were in all the provinces of King Ahasuerus, both near and far, enjoining them that they should keep the fourteenth day of the month Adar and also the fifteenth day of the same, year by year, as the days on which the Jews got relief from their enemies, and as the month that had been turned for them from sorrow into gladness and from mourning into a holiday; that they should make them days of feasting and gladness, days for sending choice portions to one another and gifts to the poor.

(Esther, IX: 20-22)

The high point of the festival comes on the fourteenth and the fifteenth of Adar. Starting at the beginning of the month, children prepare effigies of Haman and his family. Under the supervision of their teachers, they make expeditions into the fields to gather twigs. On the way, they sing passages from the Book of Esther, and if they meet "an enemy" on the road, have special couplets reserved for him.

Haman, al majbun,	Haman, who is buried,
Yekun marhum,	May he really be dead.
Haman al makhnuq,	Haman, who is choked,
Yekun mahruq.	May he be scorched.
Haman, al hazin,	Haman, who is sad,
Rijlathu fi-tin.	May his foot be under clay.
Haman, al mahruq	Haman, who is scorched,
Rijlathu fis-suq	May his foot be in the market.

On the thirteenth, men and women alike observe the fast of Esther. On the following morning, in the streets of the Hara, the effigies of Haman, his wife and his ten children are placed in bags filled with paper and wood. The children set fire to them, beat them with fronds, and sing of their destruction. They then return home and put on new clothing — but blacken their foreheads to avoid arousing envy — and they go to Houmt Souk where the adults buy them toys.

The scroll of Esther is read first at the synagogue, and then again at home for the women of the household. And just as Mordecai, the Jewish counselor of King Ahasuerus, was paraded around Susa in royal garments and on a royal mount, so too does one young jeweler drive around Hara Kebira in a splendid horse-carriage, rented especially for the occasion.

As is the case with other festivals, women participate in the ritual mainly through the preparation of food. In the days preceding Purim, they bake cakes, especially "Haman's ears." Each part of the day has its traditional culinary requirements. The meal on Purim evening consists of meats, cooked beans, and hardboiled eggs. The next morning, fritters are eaten with beans and for lunch or dinner, a *ma'qud* made of meat, eggs, flour and vegetables is prepared. Purim is the day for exchanging dishes. People send cakes to the families with whom they are close, and mothers send portions of ma'qud to their married daughters.

In the synagogue, the reading of the scroll of Esther is preceded by a collection of money. On the Saturday before Purim, the rabbi traditionally announces the amount of the tax to be levied on the community: one-half shekel of silver, the equivalent of more than four grams, for each male child. This levy is collected on the day of Purim. Half of the proceeds go toward helping the poor to celebrate Passover.

In the afternoon, the streets of Hara Kebira, all decorated for the holiday, fill up with people. The Jews of Dighet come and so do the Muslims. All of them play games of chance — usually forbidden by the rabbi — tombola, dice, cards, games with date pits. From the safety of the threshholds of their houses, even the women participate in these games. The children, whether or not they are Jewish, receive money. People eat and drink "until they can't tell Haman's blessing from Mordechai's curse."

Purim marks the changing of the seasons and puts an end to winter's confinement. Purim is the festival of inversion, of the breaking of taboos, of reversal of the norm, in which victims are transformed into victors. It is tempting to see this festival in which life triumphs over death, as the Judaization of a nature festival, and to see the rejoicings as the equivalent of carnival. But there is also a political dimension in the simulated victory of the weakest among the weak, that of the children, over the fearsome Haman.

In any case, Purim divides the year into two. As soon as it is over, preparations start immediately for the intensive three-week festive period beginning with the first day of the month of Nisan and continuing to the end of Passover on the twenty-second day of that month. Like the autumn cycle at the beginning of the year, these spring holidays have both an agricultural and a historical character. Only the themes of individual redemption and repentance, so central in the autumn festivals, are absent in the spring. The first day, *Rosh Hodesh Nisan*, is celebrated as an abbreviated version of Rosh ha-Shanah and is marked, in Jerba, by cusoms unknown to any other Jewish community, except for the one in neighboring Tripoli in Libya. A festive meal is the occasion for bringing together all members of the family. This meal is as rich and lavish as that of the Sabbath, with hardboiled eggs, beans and a couscous. Its most important moment is the ceremony of the bsisa which follows the meal. This bsisa is a porridge made from the mixed grains of several cereals — wheat, barley, sorghum — which are ground into flour and combined with a variety of spices, herbs and sugar. A large bowl of this flour is brought to the table together with a flask of olive oil. While the head of the family pours oil onto the individual plates, each member of the family puts his finger under this stream of oil. The senior male of the family then blends the oil and flour with a key, while pronouncing an invocation in Arabic:

Ya tahrik al-bsis	Oh, he who stirs the bsisa
Bel meftah wa bghair meftah	With a key or without a key
Han 'alina, ya Rebbi-l-fatah	Have mercy upon us, oh glorious God.

Every member of the family performs the same ritual, the women with a hollow, female key, the men with a full key, and all recite the same prayer. Some of the porridge is eaten immediately, and the rest is kept for the following day when, in addition, gold jewels are placed in the dish.

According to the Jerbans, this is a historical festival recalling the inauguration of the first Israelite altar in the desert. This is why Libyan Jews used to eat the very same porridge whenever they consecrated a new home. It is also a festival of nature in which, just as at Rosh ha-Shanah, prophylactic and propitiatory elements are present. The keys open the doors of plenty, while the porridge presages fertility and sweetness, and the jewels promise wealth. A particularly fortunate combination occurs when the first of Nisan falls on a Thursday, the fifth day of the week. This is the moment for writing or engraving protective charms and amulets.

Several elements of the bsisa ceremony seem to signify a seal, a finality to the outgoing year. The part of the bsisa which has not been eaten is considered *hames*, that is, leavened food which cannot be consumed during Passover and is destroyed on that account. The first of Nisan therefore anticipates part of the Passover ritual, namely the burning of the hames, the destruction of the last leavening from the preceding harvest. One other element of the festival, present also at Rosh ha-Shanah and again at Passover, is particularly noteworthy. The celebration is closed. It excludes the outside and is conceived as a way of preserving and protecting the totality of the family. Some households keep a permanent place reserved for the bsisa ceremony. Women do not allow anyone to enter or leave while they are preparing the grains for this porridge. Some prepare them at night, sheltered from other people's glances. Bsisa is not shared beyond the immediate family and people avoid going into a house where they know that it has just been made. All members of the family gather together to celebrate the ceremony, but no stranger is allowed to participate. Some people do not leave their seat from the moment the bsisa is brought to the table until the end of the evening. Though it does not have the elements of sacrifice or religious awe and devotion to God characteristic of Yom Kippur, Rosh Hodesh Nisan does manifest the symbols of the preservation and continuity of life.

Passover, the most important and the most ancient of the Jewish holidays, falls on the 14th of Nisan.

> Observe the month of Abib, and keep the Passover to the Lord your God; for in the month of Abib the Lord your God brought you out of Egypt by night. And you shall offer the Passover sacrifice to the Lord your God, from the flock or the herd, at the place which the Lord will choose, to make his name dwell there. You shall eat no leavened bread with it; seven days you shall eat it with unleavened bread, the bread of affliction — for you came out of the land of Egypt in hurried flight — that all the days of your life you may remember the day when you came out of the land of Egypt. No leaven shall be seen with you in all your territory for seven days; nor shall any of the flesh which you sacrifice in the evening of the first day remain all night until morning. You may not offer the Passover sacrifice within any of your towns which the Lord your God gives you; but at the place which the Lord your God will choose, to make His name dwell in it, there you shall offer the Passover sacrifice, in the evening at the going down of the sun, at the time you came out of Egypt. And you shall boil it and eat at the place which the Lord your God will choose; and in the morning you shall turn and go to your tents. For six days you shall eat unleavened bread; and on the seventh day there shall be a solemn assembly to the Lord your God; you shall do no work on it. You shall count seven weeks; begin to count the seven weeks from the time you first put the sickle to the standing grain. Then you shall keep the feast of weeks to the Lord your God with the tribute of a freewill offering from your hand, which you shall give as the Lord your God blesses you.
>
> (Deuteronomy, XVI: 1-10)

As a spring festival — probably its original significance — Passover is characterized by the sacrifice of a lamb. As an agricultural festival, it marks the symbolic exhaustion of the preceding year's crops through the destruction of all leavened food and the offer of the first fruit of the new harvest to God with the barley sheaf of the 'omer serving as a sacrifice. Passover is, above all, the celebration of release from bondage. As a historical festival, it employs the symbols of its more archaic levels, but reinterprets and modifies their meaning. The unleavened bread evokes the Jews' haste to leave Egypt, the herbs, the bitterness of their servitude. In Jerba, as in other Jewish communities, these elements intermingle. But whereas in other places the festival of Passover takes place in the hidden space of the house, and prayer emphasizes the memory of the exodus from Egypt, the Jerbans are still in a position to enact the various scenes of the drama in public, and to celebrate their multiple liberation from captivity: the end of winter seclusion, the first harvest and collective redemption.

In the first phase of preparations for the festival, everything in the house is renewed. On the day after Purim or, at the very latest, on the first of Nisan, the houses are whitewashed and cleaned from top to bottom. The women carry household effects to the sea, or else to a cistern outside the village, to wash them. At the beginning of the month, people also begin to prepare the grains which they will need for the eight days of Passover. Each family brings its wheat to the mill, and then prepares the dough for its unleavened bread which is baked in specially prepared communal ovens.

All kitchen utensils are thoroughly cleaned, and made *halal*, pure for use during Passover. On the thirteenth of Nisan, every trace of leavening from the preceding season is removed.

One member of the community is charged with overseeing the task of purifying the household utensils. This takes place in public, in front of each house. The utensils are heated until they glow. Immediately afterwards, those who can afford to do so have a lamb slaughtered in commemoration of the paschal sacrifice. The community's *Comité* distributes meat, rice and unleavened bread (*matzot*) to the poor families. Those who are less poor receive more discrete forms of aid from one of several informal charitable associations which operate in the Hara. Finally, in every household the last pieces of bread are collected for burning.

The two evenings of the Passover seders are not noticeably different from the ones known to other Jews, with the exception of the bulb of garlic with seven cloves which the Jerbans add to the ritual platter, and the pod with seven beans which is later hung on one of the walls of the house as a protection against scorpions. The reading of the *haggadah* and its associated customs are also similar to what other Jews know, except for the long kiddush with which the Jerbans begin the seder.

On the second day of Passover, the hind part of the lamb is roasted after a specialist has removed the nerve which would have made it unclean for eating. According to local exegetes, this roast meat commemorates the meal which Esther prepared for Ahasuerus and Haman. In the middle of the week, the association of gravediggers holds a banquet to which wine has been contributed by every household in the community. The members slaughter a lamb which they eat at this banquet, and the rabbi, who takes part in this meal, delivers a sermon to them.

On the last day, after the afternoon prayer, the children go out into the streets and loudly announce that the festival is over. They disguise a man, paint his face and lead him from house to house reciting couplets which predict prosperity for the coming season. At each stop, they receive wine from the master of the house, along with biscuits and dried fruit. Once night has fallen, the Muslims bring fish and the first leavening for the next day's meal.

Throughout this entire eight day period — just as at Rosh ha-Shanah and on the first of Nisan — the Jerbans are doubly closed off, both from other Jewish families and from non-Jews. Whereas in other parts of the world, Jewish families usually gather together to celebrate Passover in common (leaving the door open for whoever is hungry and looking for shelter is an almost universal Passover custom), the Jerbans keep their doors closed. They attribute this usage to the experience of the Marranos in Spain where the Christians recognized the secret practices of the converted Jews by their observance of the Passover seder. In remembrance of their persecution, Passover is celebrated in isolation. Another explanation goes as follows: one day, when a stranger had been taken into a Jerban household, he suddenly took out a loaf of bread and put it on the table, thereby desecrating the premises. Both of these stories imply that Passover means the separation and the suspension of secular activities. Exchanges with outsiders, which are very brisk during the preceding week when Muslim merchants bring all the foodstuffs necessary for the eight days of the festival, are suspended during Passover. The Jews do not buy anything. They close their shops and take a vacation for the entire week, abandoning all economic exchange. Life resumes its normal course when the Muslims bring the leavening which marks the end of the Passover restrictions.

The Jerban version of the *mimuna* (which follows immediately after the end of Passover) must be understood in this context. Among the Moroccan Jews, who attach a particular importance to this custom, the mimuna combines many elements. It is a picnic outside of the area in which one usually lives. It involves exchanges of visits and greetings among Jewish families and the consumption of dishes which presage a good year. Before the Jewish exodus from Morocco, the mimuna also encompassed exchanges with Muslims who brought bread, vegetables and sweets and took away with them a promise of fertility for their own harvests. And finally, the mimuna is a ritual of inversion, with little girls dressing up as Muslim women, and men disguising themselves as women.[3]

In Jerba, a number of these same features are present but are disconnected. On the "night of the mimuna," young men do go out to the countryside, but no picnic takes place. Instead, they cut branches from olive trees and exchange greetings by tapping each other on the shoulder while wishing one another life and peace. Unlike its Moroccan counterpart, the masquerade does not belong to the ritual of mimuna. This element is displaced to the last day of Passover when the children drag a man in disguise from house to house. Finally, the mimuna meal is supposed to assure the transition to ordinary food. According to some, it consists of a couscous made with wheat bought before the holiday, or with a flour made by grinding the Passover matzot. This main dish is accompanied by vegetables which may be eaten during the holiday, and a portion of the paschal lamb. It therefore brings together all the elements of the Passover week. According to others, the meal consists of bread baked in the house oven, and eaten with dried fruit, wine, fat from the sacrificial lamb, eggs and garlic. This dish bears the name of *qlayia*. In either case, in order to safeguard one's good fortune, the meal must be consumed in its entirety. Nothing is to be left over and not a crumb is to be dropped on the ground.

For the kohanim of Dighet, who add three additional days to the eight days of Passover, there is a different version of the mimuna. Because of its name it is connected to an incident in the life of Maimonides. A Muslim baker once put poison in the bread he prepared for the Jews immediately after Passover. In a dream, Maimonides received a warning about this from the prophet Elijah. He therefore decreed that the Passover should be prolonged by a day. However, the baker persisted in his evil machinations for three days. Finally, the Sultan intervened and insisted that the Jews pay for the three oven-loads of bread which had been lost. Maimonides accepted on condition that the baker eat some of his own bread first. He ate some and died.

Every ritual implies the separation and isolation of those who take part in it. The mimuna meal, which is a kind of summation of everything which has been eaten during Passover, prolongs this separation before contact is resumed with non-Jews and with secular life which, in the story, are symbolized by the evil baker and the poisoned bread.

In all of these rituals, there is a kind of redundancy. Just as Rosh ha-Shanah is mirrored in Rosh Hodesh Nisan, just as the fire is rekindled on the tomb of Sidi Youssef al-Ma'rabi, so Passover is celebrated, in a reduced version, on the fourteenth of *Iyyar*. Unleavened bread, which has been kept for this second Passover, is eaten then. This same day commemorates the hillula of Rabbi Meir Ba'l Ha-nes followed by that of Rabbi Shim'on bar Yohai (known throughout North Africa as Rebbi Shem'un) on the eighteenth of Iyyar. For these celebrations, the Ghriba becomes the center of ritual activity.

From the second day of Passover — the day on which one offers to God the first barley sheaf, the 'omer — until the sixth of *Sivan*, the Jews observe seven weeks of mourning, interrupted only between the 14th and the 18th of Iyyar. During this time of mourning no on may shave, no weddings may take place, houses cannot be whitewashed, and no new ventures should be undertaken. The mourning period ends on Shavu'oth, which manifests the same kind of ambivalence as the other festivals. On the one hand, it marks the end of the harvest which began in the month of Nisan. Jews eat and exchange all sorts of roasted grains and pulses — flax, chickpeas, lentils, beans, wheat and barley. On the other hand, it recalls Moses receiving the Torah on Mount Sinai. The women make pastries for the children, in many different shapes, such as the ladder on which Moses climbed Mount Sinai, the hand which received the Tablets of the Law, the birds, the messengers of peace, who surrounded Moses, and so on. On the Saturday before Shavu'oth, the rabbi pronounces a drash on the merits of studying the Law, and funds are pledged for the *Or Torah* (Light of the Torah) Society which supports the community's educational activities. The night of Shavu'oth is spent in prayer and study. The Ten Commandments are read in Hebrew and in Arabic translation, and are commented on in both languages. In the morning, the children run through the streets to sell the texts of charms which will protect the household against scorpions.

During the following weeks, corresponding to the month of June and the beginning of July, the atmosphere becomes more relaxed, with no rituals, no prohibitions, and no penance. Weddings take place. This respite does not last long. Beginning with the 17th of Tammuz, the Jerbans once again enter a prolonged period of mourning, followed by repentance, interrupted only by a break of ten days. This period of mourning leads to and prepares the following year's period of judgement.

> Then he brought me to the entrance of the north gate of the house of the Lord; and behold there sat women weeping for Tammuz.
>
> (Ezekiel 8:14)

In Babylonian tradition, Tammuz is the son (or the spouse?) of the goddess Ishtar, who went down to the nether world in the fourth month of the year and stayed there until the following spring. Tammuz symbolized spring greenery, and his disappearance was marked by a period of mourning in Babylon. Among the Jews, the public fast of the 17th of Tammuz and its mourning rituals are very likely remnants of this cult. But here again, historical commemoration has obscured the nature cult. On the 17th of Tammuz, Moses shattered the Tablets of the Law. It is also the day on which the defenses of Jerusalem began to falter under the pressure of the Roman legions. After the public fast of the 17th of Tammuz, the Jerbans observe various aspects of mourning for a three week period. Men do not shave; people wear old clothes, and no weddings take place. Mourning intensifies from the first to the ninth of Av. People stop eating meat, even on the Sabbath; they are not allowed to wash, nor to cut their hair, nor to travel, nor to undertake any new ventures. On the ninth, the mourning culminates with another public fast.

From the 17th of Tammuz until the 9th of Av, the men gather daily at the synagogue around noon-time and, seated on the bare ground (another sign of mourning), they chant lamentations. On the eve of the 9th of Av, they add poems and songs to the usual prayers. On the afternoon of the ninth, during the fast, they gather again in the synagogues to sing dirges, *qinot*. The best-known dirge is the one about Hannah and her seven sons, each of whom perishes before her eyes because he refuses to deny his faith by bowing down before other gods.

The women also sing dirges, and refrain from sewing and doing the wash during the ten days of mourning. They banish meat from their tables, and prepare a ritual meal for the Saturday before the 9th of Av, the *shimshuma*, based on lentils and dry grains. On the ninth of the month in Dighet, some of them go to the cemetery with the professional mourners, and, bent over in the shade of a wall, they let out terrifying wails as they beat their own bodies.

This three week period of mourning is one of the rare occasions when the young girls of the community have a specific and active role in the ritual scenario. Throughout these three weeks, they gather every evening at dusk to sing dirges in Arabic. There is one about Hannah and her seven sons, and another about a young girl whom a pagan king desired to take to wife, but who escaped this unwelcome marriage by transforming herself into a night bird, the *buma*. The longest dirge tells the story of a young Jewish girl who bravely repels the advances of the non-Jew who wants to marry her.

> She was washing clothes, ya'ouilia,
> A son of a Christian passed by, ya'ouilia,
> He said to her, "Whose daughter are you?"
> She said to him, "A daughter of Israel."
> "If only I could take one of you!"
> "May He not leave you alive on that day!
> Your religion is that of the Christians,
> Our is the religion of Moses and the Law."

Except for one of these songs, which lists all the kinds of grain and which, like the shimshuma, refers to the seasonal death of vegetation, all of these qinot (dirges) share the theme of refusal pushed to the limit of sacrifice.

On the Friday preceding the ninth of Av, the girls are awakened very early, since starting their household tasks early on this day assures their diligence for the entire year. On the same day, the children walk under the olive trees and throw balls of wool at the top of the trees. These are intended for the buma, the bird with a human face who wanders around the ruins. In this game, the girls ask for beauty, white skin, and proficiency at their household tasks. On the ninth of Av, the boys arm themselves with bows and shoot arrows at the sky. They fly kites and spin weathervanes. These are games which local interpretations relate, not without difficulty, to the struggle against the Romans, but which seem, more simply, to be linked to the movement of the sun and stars. The same applies to the practice which, for the girls, consists of making figurines out of pearls — or, in days gone by, out of lentils and other pulses — on the morning of the ninth of Av, before sunrise. "To bring back the sun," says one of them, "to repair the limbs of the Jewish soldiers who died during the defense of the Temple," correct the others.

After the fast, the rabbi shares a pumpkin with the men at the synagogue. The 15th of Av is a good time for wearing new clothes and making purchases, and for starting new ventures. Five days later, the 20th day of Av inaugurates the series of encounters during which the men ask each other to be freed from their unfulfilled engagements. At every midnight of the month of Elul, the slihot — supplications — are recited in synagogues. Someone goes from door to door calling the faithful together in preparation for the judgement which comes with the following month.

As we asserted at the outset of this chapter, time in Jerba is full and being a Jew in Jerba is a full-time activity. The preceding pages are by no means a complete inventory of all the rituals, customs and practices which the Jews of Jerba have devised to accompany almost every moment of their lives, nor have they done full justice to the vitality and zeal with which they continue to be observed and applied. Other Jews, especially those of North Africa, have passed through a process of secularization which, when not displacing religious practice entirely, has isolated it from other activities. Losing its original purpose, the synagogue became simply a place for individual devotions, and religious practice was transformed into a domestic cult. The communal dimension disappeared. Not so for the Jews of Jerba. Collective rhythms continue to powerfully dominate their community and any separation between the public and the private is indistinct. Though the symbolism of their practices is not always clear, practical knowledge about how to perform them is inculcated in all members of the community, and all share the same practical memory.

In other parts of North Africa, it was possible to assert: "Rites take place, and they only take place because they find their *raison d'être* in the conditions of existence and in the dispositions of agents who cannot afford the luxury of logical speculation, of mystical effusion or of metaphysical anxiety."[4] For the Jews of Jerba, mystical effusion and metaphysical anxiety are not a luxury, but a condition of their lives.

1.   Jews in the diaspora celebrate Rosh ha-Shanah for two days. The same is true for the first days of Succoth, Passover and Shavu'oth.
2.   A prayer, consisting in the main of selections from the Psalms, recited on the major holidays.
3.   H. E. GOLDBERG, "The Mimuna and Minority Status of Moroccan Jews", *Ethnology*, 17 (1978), pp. 75-88.
4.   P. BOURDIEU, "Le sens pratique," *Actes de la Recherche en Sciences Sociales*, February, 1976, pp. 43-86.

5
Ahl al-Kitāb
People of the Book

Solitary study
before the evening
services.

In the *yeshiva*: a teacher explaining a Talmudic passage to his pupils.

Islam designates the followers of revealed religions as *ahl al-kitab*, people of the book. In its domains, there is no group which has so well deserved this appellation as the Jews of Jerba.

Over the past hundred years, the Jewish community of this island has produced close to five hundred published books. Because of the informal, disorganized nature of this activity, the exact number is nearly impossible to establish and it might, in reality, be much higher. These are published books and the figure does not include works still in manuscript form. Some of the latter are of very recent date, just completed or still in the course of being written; others date back a century or more and are part of the literary production of scholars, rabbis and learned laymen, some of whose works have already been published. These manuscripts are in the hands of the descendants of the authors and there is a good likelihood that many of them will be printed at one time or another. It is also likely that more books will be written in Jerba, although probably not nearly at the same rate as in the past half century. In addition to books, for two decades, beginning in the mid-30's, there were between three and five monthly journals published and written in Jerba.

Before the twentieth century, the literary output of Jerban scholars was published either in Leghorn, Tunis or Jerusalem. In 1903, a Hebrew printing press was imported to Jerba, and since that date, virtually every work in that language or in Judeo-Arabic written on the island and in its allied communities of Southern Tunisia (Gabes, Zarzis, Ben Gardane, Tatahouine, Medenine) was published in Jerba. Jerba also became the publishing center for religious literary works from other parts of North Africa.

These data would be of little significance or interest if it were not for the fact that the community we are talking about numbered, for most of this period, between 2000 and 3000 people; that for only a brief period in the 1940's and early 1950's did it approach 5,000 souls, and that, until recently, none of its women could read or write. Furthermore,

At Al-Hammá near Gabes. A Jerban reading a prayer specific to this pilgrimage.

this is a community in which more than 90% of the males earn their livelihood by the sweat of their brow. While many of the Jewish (not necessarily Hebrew) books written and published in Jerba were authored by "professionals," that is, by full-time rabbis or religious teachers, many were written by laymen, by men whose weekdays were spent in the market-place or in their workshops.

This impressive level of literary productivity is unusual, and, with the exception of such specialized communities as academia, may be unprecedented. The fact that for the past century or so the Jews of this island devoted such a disproportionate amount of their time, energy and resources to the composition and publication of books certainly needs an explanation. What is it that they wrote? Why did they write it? For whom? To answer these questions one must begin by describing two complementary phenomena: the place of traditional learning in the Jerban Jewish community, and the community's vision of itself and its own local religious traditions and customs.

Study

Since the destruction of the Temple in Jerusalem, God's spirit has found no other resting place except in the four cubits of the study of religious law (*arba' amot shel halakha*).

This passage from the Talmud is frequently cited by Jews from Jerba to explain the place of religious studies in their community. Thus, the purpose of study is not merely to ascertain God's will or a supplemental form of serving God, but also to provide the only suitable and tranquil home for God before the reconstruction of the Temple. Jerban Jews share with traditional Jews everywhere the same high regard for the study of Torah. What sets Jerban

85

Jews apart is the fervor and consistency with which they have constructed a multi-roomed mansion for God's repose.

Underpinning this entire structure is a comprehensive educational system which does not simply ensure the community's instructional needs. It also integrates within it many of the values which have permitted the community to resist outside influence and maintain itself. From its inception it touched upon many other non-educational aspects of the community's structure and values. For the Jewish male population of Jerba, the traditional system of education is both universal and compulsory; until quite recently it was also exclusive of all others. It was the only one available to the young males of the Hara Kebira. This system of traditional instruction (Bible, Talmud, Commentaries, prayers, religious law) occupied every eligible young man for an average of ten years of his life between the age of four and fourteen for twelve hours a day, every day of the year except for Sabbaths and holidays. Both the content of the educational system and its fierce exclusivity date back to the last years of the 19th and early years of the 20th century. These developed as part of a vigorous response in opposition to the various attempts from external sources to introduce modern, western-oriented schools into the community, and resulted in the establishment of an educational system under exclusive indigenous control. This exclusivity was breached, and then only partially, in very recent years. Since it is the educational policy of the Jerban Jewish community which is perhaps more than any other single factor responsible for its remarkable survival and cultural integrity, it is worthwhile devoting some attention to these events.

In 1894 or 1895, on the initiative of Rabbi Moshe Khalfon Hacohen (1874-1950), who was later to become the most influential rabbinic figure of Jerban Judaism, a fund to support the study of the Torah was inaugurated in Jerba. Its announced aim was "to spread and strengthen the study of the Torah in Jerba" by making such study accessible to every male child in the community. Until less than two decades ago, religious education was a private affair. Most of the synagogues of the Hara housed teachers and rabbis who offered instruction to youngsters in return for a weekly fee paid by their parents. For many poor families, this was a heavy economic burden; for some it was too heavy. The new fund undertook to pay the tuition fees of any and all needy students, to provide them with books, and to offer subsidies to their families. As a consequence, it made Jewish religious education universal in the community. The revenues for support of this enterprise derived from several sources. Collection boxes, with notices enjoining the congregants to offer a small sum each day, were placed in the synagogues of the Hara which were regularly frequented by virtually all its adult males. A group of more well-to-do citizens undertook to contribute a fixed weekly amount to the fund — a kind of regular voluntary tax. In addition, contributions were solicited at all festive occasions such as circumcisions and weddings, as well as at special services celebrating some personal thanksgiving, or prophylactic services in cases of illness or other misfortunes. One of the special Sabbaths of the year, *shabbat kallah*, which precedes the holidays of *Shavu'oth*, was set aside for an appeal in all synagogues of the village for contributions to this fund.

This mode of recruiting students and financing their studies transformed an educational project into a civic enterprise. In a very short time, the fund achieved popular success and realized its initial goals. In 1918 it changed its name to *Or Torah* (the Light of the Torah Society), expanded its structure and broadened and elaborated its program. It included within its purview an entire range of communal functions, such as the education and training of teachers, rabbis, scribes, ritual slaughterers and Torah readers for Jerba and for its satellite communities in South Tunisia. Beyond the minimal religious training of youngsters from poor families, it now sought to encourage advanced study beyond the age of thirteen for any promising scholars by providing support, prizes and incentives to both diligent students and effective teachers. If a young man was prepared to continue his religious training until his late teens or early twenties, and then seek a secular profession, the society undertook to subsidize his training and apprenticeship. In practice, the impact of the Or Torah Society went far beyond its original educational goals. "Spreading and strengthening the study of the Torah" became one of the most effective means of the community's cultural and religious reproduction. It guaranteed a uniform training for all men, their full participation in religious activities, gave rise to a stable learned elite, and provided a pool of trained communal professionals.

The success, effectiveness and longevity of the Or Torah Society are remarkable from another point of view. In its social life over the past century, Jerban Judaism generated very few stable, articulated community-wide structures or institutions. The Or Torah Society was an exception. It elicited wide and continuing material support, in the form of contributions and endowments which at times resembled a voluntary taxation system. In social and cultural terms, the community — in many other ways fragmented and litigious — developed a consensus in support of this society's goals of strengthening religious study.

The Or Torah Society still exists and functions, albeit at a much reduced level. Even now the revenue from its collection boxes and the annual campaigns exceeds 1000 dinars (approximately $2500). The Society sponsored a journal of religious studies which appeared irregularly in Jerba but which now appears regularly as a monthly journal in Israel. It is run by Jerban Jews and publishes the scholarly insights of learned Jerban Jews, as well as stories and tales of their rabbis.

The group dedicated to strengthening religious education thus integrated many other community values and concerns, and it can be said without fear of exaggeration, that for the past 75 years, it integrated the entire community within its program. The Jewish religious leadership, undermined and obsolete in the rest of Tunisia, forcefully maintained its monopoly over the local educational system. It rejected secular education under the auspices of the French colonial authorities. The French government school, built on its outskirts, was totally boycotted by the residents of the Hara. Neither the pressure emanating from Jewish notables in Tunis and from the local French governor, nor threats and the use of force — youngsters were pulled out of their synagogue schools by cavalrymen and conducted to the French school while their parents were dragged before magistrates in Houmt Souk — were of any avail. Only a handful of youths from families permanently settled in Houmt Souk dared attend this public school.

With equal, if not greater, vehemence did the religious leadership in Jerba exclude and suppress any effort to introduce secular or foreign elements into their educational system, even under specifically Jewish auspices. In 1904 a violent controversy erupted over this very issue. The *Alliance Israélite Universelle* was a Paris-based organization dedicated to improving the condition of the Jews of North Africa and the Levant through modern education and training. Its educational system was patterned on the French secular model, and the aim of its schools was to prepare Jewish youngsters for the "emancipation" already enjoyed by their coreligionists in Europe. By 1904, the Alliance had founded several schools in Tunisia without running into much difficulty. At Hara Kebira, its representatives encountered implacable and, as it turned out, insurmountable resistance. They proposed the establishment of a school exclusively for Jewish children that would respect traditional practices and values, that would teach Hebrew and religion, but that would also offer instruction in French language and in general educational subjects. The local French authorities endorsed the project wholeheartedly as did some Jewish families of Italian origin. The rabbis of Jerba, however, perceived this proposal as threat and a profanation. In response to the challenge of a French government school, they had declared a simple boycott. Reacting to this menace, they proclaimed a solemn ban of excommunication against any member of the community who collaborated with the Alliance by providing a building for the proposed school or by agreeing to send their children to be educated in it. This ban is constantly recalled and its text is reproduced in Rabbi Moshe Khalfon Hacohen's *Brith Kehuna*, the authoritative compilation of Jerban Jewish customs.

Significantly, this ban did not extend to the proposed government school but only to a school intended specifically and exclusively for Jews. The latter was viewed as a far greater menace to the integrity of the community than the former. In justifying and defending their relentless opposition to an Alliance school in Jerba, the rabbis constantly pointed to the ominous precedent of Tunis, where, in their view, the introduction of an Alliance-type education for Jews had led to a precipitous decline in Jewish religious knowledge and, more importantly, religious observance.

The rejection of the Alliance school represented a critical choice for the Jews of Jerba. It marked a turning point in their history and is viewed as such by them to this very day. Every Jewish adult in Jerba is familiar with the details of the struggle against the Alliance. It is recounted over and over again and has become part of their folklore and popular history because it represents the formal exclusion from their cultural horizon of foreign, nontraditional elements — a principle for which there remains a consensus in theory, if not entirely in practice, to the present.

By condemning any project of educational innovation based on the French model, without foregoing the possibility of innovation within the confines of their own tradition, the Jerban Jewish "Ulema" attained several objectives. They banished foreign elements from their immediate environment and barred contacts which might corrupt the youth. They avoided the kind of social drain which occurred in other communities because of the access to new occupations and to western-type schools. They prevented the exposure of the Jerbans to the corrosive knowledge that might come via familiarity with a foreign language and a secular education. In a large measure this strategy was successful.

It was not until the 1940's that the Jerbans were prepared to accept two basic reforms. The first was the establishment of a school which supplemented the *yeshiva* curriculum by offering instruction in modern Hebrew and in several non-religious subjects. The second, and more important, reform was the opening of this new school to girls. This was the first time in Jerba's history that any of its women attained literacy. This was the first time also that any alternative, no matter how partial, to traditional pedagogy was available. For a very small number, it made possible access to more advanced educational institutions beyond the boundaries of the community.

The rabbinic authorities did not take the initiative for these reforms. Rather, they grew out of proposals submitted to them by a group of young people inspired by the Zionist ideals then in vogue who were also promoting athletic and agricultural education. The latter proposals were rejected out of hand as incompatible with Jerban values. But the rabbis did consent to the other educational reforms with the proviso that they be adapted to local conditions. This meant the strict separation of girls and boys and the continued monopoly of the yeshiva over all religious education. Far from undermining the old system, the new school simply complemented it.

Following independence, the Jews accepted Tunisian schools. In the two Haras today, an increasing number of children of both sexes attend "the government school."

Consequently, Jews are currently involved in three educational systems. During each day, a child passes through three schools. First, the yeshiva where the instruction is in Hebrew and Judeo-Arabic, then the Tunisian public school where Arabic and also French are languages of communication and finally, the modern Jewish school for instruction in modern Hebrew. Each school has its own language, its own curriculum and its own diploma. Nevertheless, it is traditional education which continues to govern the lives of the young. Very few of them do in fact complete the high school program of the public school. Now as before most adolescents abandon their schooling at age 14 in pursuit of a livelihood. By age 14, a boy has completed the traditional core curriculum which acquaints him with Hebrew and prayers at age 5, the Pentateuch at age 7 and religious law and the Babylonian Talmud as he reaches his teens. These studies culminate with some chapters of the tractate *Baba Mesi'a* dealing with rabbinic commercial law intended to prepare boys for their careers in the marketplace.

Because they have no post-school prospect except for marriage, Jerban girls, paradoxically, now enjoy a longer period and a higher level of education in non-religious subjects than do their brothers. Several girls have actually attained the baccalaureat, the very summit of Tunisian public school education.

Literary Activity

When, at age 14, a young man leaves the yeshiva for the marketplace, his institutional possibilities for continued study do not cease. Every evening of the week, between 9:00 and 10:30 p.m., advanced classes or seminars of Talmud study used to be held at several synagogues in the Hara. At present, two such groups are still active and, at one time, more then ten were in existence. Some of these groups met for one or two hours of study each morning as well. The participants in these study groups are merchants and craftsmen of the *suq*; their text is a tractate of the Talmud with several of its major commentaries. In the course of a year, several chapters of a tractate will have been thoroughly studied and commented upon; in the course of a lifetime, several major tractates of the Talmud will have been studied at least once. For the less advanced laymen, there was, in past years, in each synagogue, a suggested program of daily study which in the course of the year would take one through all the books of the Pentateuch, Prophets and Writings as well as through some books of the Mishnah.

Involvement in study was frequently very intense. One young jeweler in Jerba — now less than thirty years old — told us the following: when he was thirteen years old, he was studying the tractate of *Hulin* and his rabbi took special pains to explain an argument of one of the twelfth-century scholastic commentators on that particular passage. In spite of his best and most ardent intentions and in spite of the repeated and patient explanations of his teacher, the boy was simply unable to grasp the fine points of the dialogue between the commentator and the Talmudic passage. So great was his distress and frustration that he burst into tears and remained inconsolable for an entire day. At age 15 or 16, the same young man began, once a week, to record in a clean white, lined notebook, his own insights and commentaries upon the text of those sections of the Talmud he was studying. He continued this practice for several years and more than a decade later had not excluded the possibility of having these youthful writings published in Jerba.

To be sure, not every Jewish craftsman in Jerba is a part-time author, nor is the zeal for learning of every student at the yeshiva equal to that of this particular young jeweler. For most boys, studying the Torah and Talmud consists of reading, in a specifically Jerban cantillation, short passages of the Hebrew or Aramaic text followed by a mechanical word-for-word translation into dialectal Arabic — a translation which they have heard from their teacher and memorized as a result of numerous oral repetitions. The level of true comprehension varies greatly. By the time most boys reach the age of twelve, one senses a distinct impatience to be done with their formal studies and to get out into the adult world by acquiring a profession or a craft. This generally takes place between the ages of thirteen and fifteen. One should hasten to add, however, that if not all the "graduates" of the yeshiva are equally learned, they are uniformly prepared to participate in all aspects of private and public ritual activities which the community consensus considers essential to its social existence and cultural continuity.

To get back to our learned jeweler: in considering the publication of his youthful Talmudic insights he was continuing a family tradition while simultaneously participating in a process of affirmation of the Jerban Jewish community's identity. Several decades earlier the comments of his paternal uncle on several Talmudic tractates were published in Jerba. The volume was printed posthumously (as is frequently the case) by the family to commemorate the premature death of their relative, who died as a comparatively young, unmarried man. Commemoration, filial and family piety, were in the past and continue in the present as strong motives for Jerban Jewish publications.

Even though, as will be discussed shortly, the circumstances and the immediate purpose of local writing and publishing may be diverse, these examples are neither isolated nor unusual. Today, there are at least twenty men in Hara Kebira who have some sort of published writing to their credit, and this at a time when the male adult population does not exceed two hundred. Some of these publications are brief, signed novellae growing out of adult study groups and printed as supplements to larger books or as contributions to the monthly religious journals which appeared during the 1940's and 1950's. Others are works of more substantial length, such as commentaries on the entire book of Psalms or the Haggadah of Passover, collections of local responsa or sermons delivered at various important occasions. At least four learned men (one of them a young jeweller less than 25 years old) are currently devoting their scholarly efforts to a peculiarly Jerban literary genre—histories of their own community, of its specific customs, its families and its rabbis. It should be noted, once again, that none of these men are "professional" writers or people who earn their living from scholarly pursuits. They are active in the world of commerce and crafts and their literary work represents the uppermost level of a cultural and educational system which, at its base, encompasses the entire community.

Publishing in Jerba

Before the twentieth century, the Jerban community was compelled to import from distant places all the Hebrew books for its educational and religious needs. The community was poor, the books expensive and their number insufficient for its requirements. The literary production of Jerban Jewish scholars was also constrained. Publication was possible only at the distant presses of Leghorn in Italy or at those of Jerusalem or Tiberias in Palestine. Publication of a manuscript involved great trouble, expense and delay. As a consequence, only a small portion of the works written actually saw the light of day. With the establishment of a Hebrew press in Jerba by Rabbi David Aydan in 1903, this situation was qualitatively transformed. Many manuscripts by leading contemporary scholars as well as those of preceding generations could be published more expeditiously. Books required for expanding the educational the religious needs of the community could be produced locally and at a reasonable expense. The first three decades of the 20th century witnessed a "golden age" of Hebrew printing in Jerba. Within a rather short time, the single press proved insufficient to meet the needs of Jerba and the demand from numerous North African Jewish communities. Other printing shops were established and, at the high point, there were five Hebrew publishing houses on the island, including one in the Hara Sghira. Of these, two are still active to this very day.

These enterprises were in no way charitable or subsidized institutions, but were commercially viable undertakings. The books they published were bought, paid for and used. The primary consumers of the books published in Jerba were the Jews of Jerba themselves and those of its satellite settlements in southern Tunisia. The next level of readership consisted of the Jewish communities of Tunisia and North Africa as a whole (Libya, Algeria and Morocco), and at a more remote level and in a more limited manner, Jews all over the world. The language of their writing was either Hebrew, the lingua franca of traditional Jewish scholarship, or Judeo-Arabic, that is, the spoken Arabic dialect of southern Tunisia tran-

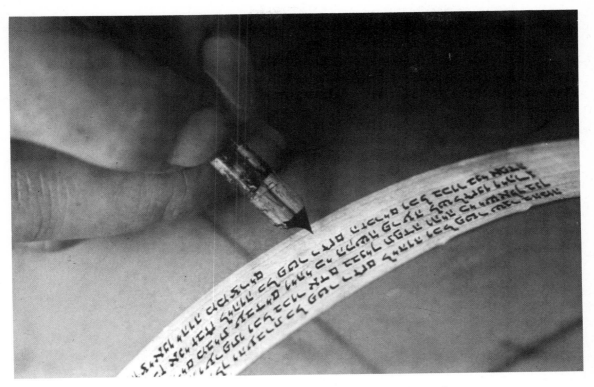

"Jerba, a city of scribes and scholars." One of several Jerban scribes
preparing a new Torah scroll on parchment.

scribed in Hebrew characters. Works composed in this dialect were, of course, totally inaccessible and of no interest to traditional Jews beyond the boundaries of Tunisia.

This distribution of Jerban books corresponds to a more general pattern of Jerban Jewish cultural identity and practice. At the very center stand the Jerban Jewish communities and their southern Tunisian satellites with their elaborate system of local customs, and their distinctive modes of linguistic, social and economic interaction with the Muslim environment. Tunisian and North African Jewry constitute the second circle with whom the Jerban Jews share, in varying degrees, a common language and general Maghrebi traditions and practices, as well as the general experience of a millennial contact with Arab-Muslim culture. With Jews the world over, the Jerban communities share a body of common religious texts, and the fervent sense of a common past and ultimately of a common destiny. Much of what they share with other Jews has, in Jerba, taken on a style and form which is specifically Jerban. This is especially true of their books which are at the same time the expression and the instrument of this distinctive Judaism formed in an Islamic milieu.

A Bookseller's Catalogue

Commentary and compilation are the dominant modes of Jerban Jewish literary activity. Originality is not the most prized quality of a Jerban Jewish book. What is sought in a book is that it be useful, reliable, and interesting; that the material be gathered from accepted sources and put together in a form that is new to Jerba and relevant to Jerban concerns, values and practices.

A partial analysis of a book catalogue issued in January, 1957 by one of the leading Hebrew publishers on the island will illustrate the variety of ways in which these concerns

A
printer's
shop.

92

are addressed. In the first section entitled "Prayer Books and Books for Laymen," seventy items — all published in Jerba — are listed. All of these books are for use in public and private worship and ritual. With some important exceptions, these are the same devotional texts which are used by Jews everywhere. It is their form, variety and some aspect of their content which made them specifically Jerban. Their format is small, so that they can easily be accommodated in a pocket or in the fold of one's sleeve. On weekdays, the three daily prayers vary substantially from one another. Sabbaths and major festivals have their own specific prayer service; there are, in addition, numerous daily, weekly and monthly occasions requiring an appropriate prayer or blessing. To fill these needs, the printer offers a choice of remarkable variety to suit every conceivable taste and inclination. There are prayer books which contain only the morning prayers for the weekdays, others containing the afternoon and evening prayers, others still which add to these the corresponding service for the Sabbath and holidays. One advertised prayerbook is designed especially for travellers, and others contain separate texts for individual festivals or special occasions. All of these contain parenthetical instructions and summaries of the rules of prayer in the Judeo-Arabic dialect of Jerba. Some examples:

Seder Hodesh Nisan — (Order of the Month of Nisan) — Jerba, n.d. Rules pertaining to the spring month of Nisan at the mid-point of which the festival of Passover occurs. It includes prayers and customs associated with each day of the month as well as the rules — in Judeo-Arabic — concerning Passover and the preparation of the seder and the various dishes required for this ritual meal. In addition there is a commentary on the ethical significance of these rules and a collection of *piyyutim* — poems in both Hebrew and Arabic which are to be sung or recited at various points in the ceremony.

Sefer Tefila u-Tehina — (A Book of Prayer and Supplication) — A collection of special poems and prayers of mourning (*tiqqunim* and *qinot*) for the four minor fast days. Also included is a summary in Judeo-Arabic of the rules pertaining to these fast days.

Sefer Yom Hazikaron — (Book for the Day of Remembrance) — Jerba, 1945. A 53-page pamphlet containing the text of prayers for select ceremonies connected with the New Year and Yom Kippur. Some of the ceremonies are specific to Jerba and are not practised in any other Jewish communities. The version of some of the prayers, including the *kol nidre*, the most famous prayer on the Eve of Yom Kippur — is one which is recited only in certain synagogues of Jerba, and nowhere else.

Tefilot — (Prayers) — Jerba, 1938. An eleven page pamphlet containing two prayers: first, the awesome prayer of Rabbi Ishmael the High Priest ("anyone who says this prayer every day will be spared all evil events,") and second, a prayer to be recited each day against the evil eye.

As we have noted elsewhere, being a Jew in Jerba is a full-time activity. For the adult males, most of these activities are accompanied by an obligatory blessing, prayer or ceremony. Of all the ceremonial requirements of traditional Jews everywhere, nothing is omitted and nothing is forgotten. On the contrary, numerous local and regional additions have accumulated over the ages. On the Sabbath eve, the head of the household does not simply recite the special blessing over the wine — which is all that is strictly required by Jewish religious law. In Jerba the blessing is preceded and followed by the declamation of several fairly lengthy poems and prayers. A similar pattern repeats itself for other Sabbath and festival ceremonies.

Since praying is not only an act of individual piety but is also an affirmation of ethnic and communal identity, this variety of prayer books becomes a necessity. Their production and printing are more than just a commercial enterprise. They are a response to a social need.

The same holds true for the production of scholarly books. Here again, the individual intellectual effort is embedded within its communal context. In the 1957 book catalogue mentioned above, we encounter a major rubric entitled: Books for Learned Men (*Talmidei Hakhamim*). Of the 86 books listed under this heading, 57 were authored and printed in Jerba. Of these, the largest category consists of commentaries on the Bible and the Talmud, 16 on the Bible and 14 on the Talmud. Nine books are collections of sermons and there are four separate editions of the Haggadah of Passover, each with its own commentary by a Jerban Jewish scholar. Religious poetry, legal responsa, law and customs are the subject matter of the other books in this category.

Each type of book is associated with a community institution of prayer or study or commemoration. Commentaries on the Bible concentrate on the Pentateuch — i.e., the Torah. In the course of a year, as part of the Sabbath service, the entire Torah, from Genesis to Deuteronomy, is read in the synagogue in weekly portions. On Friday mornings, the portion of the week is reviewed by all the children in the yeshiva, and on Saturday afternoons many adult males gather in the synagogue to study the portion of the week individually or in groups. The text of the Bible and its commentaries are intimately familiar to many in the community and, as a consequence, the authors are as likely to be learned laymen as "professional" scholars.

Collections of homilies (*drash*), as independent books or as supplements to other works also spring from an institutional context. One Saturday afternoon a month, a rabbi delivers an address at the Great Synagogue for the entire community. Major holidays are another occasion for homilies, as are special commemorations for deceased rabbis or revered personalities of the past. After a man's death, a different homily by a different person is offered in honor of the deceased every day of the following week in the home of the bereaved family. These are wide-ranging, with elaborate interpretations of Talmudic passages combined with exegesis of Biblical verses and edifying stories and exhortations to charity, piety and sincere religious observance. Delivering these sermons — whether in the synagogue or elsewhere — is not a professional rabbinic prerogative, but is the informal privilege of any learned, respected member of the community who, regardless of his actual profession, is, by virtue of his learning and comportment, entitled to the designation "Rabbi." Unlike most other forms of scholarly writing (the other major exception being the legal responsa), the language of the homilies is Judeo-Arabic and not Hebrew. It is, thus, a semi-popular form of writing; the religious knowledge and ideas it contains are accessible to wider circles of males who cannot easily follow the intricacies, refinements and copious cross-references of the locally-produced and locally-favored commentaries on the Talmud.

Commentaries on the Talmud take pride of place in the literary activity of Jerban Jews. No Jerban scholar has composed a commentary on the entire Talmud. The preferred form is rather a collection of scholia, comments and insights on a single, or at most two or three tractates of the Babylonian Talmud. These comments are generated either by teaching or the organized study (at the yeshiva or at one of the evening study "seminars") of the particular text. It has often been said that scholarship is a lonely activity. This is true in Jerba as well. But here again we observe a communal institution, a social stimulus even for the most sophisticated form of scholarship.

Place, Time and Learning

In 1896, one of the leading families of Hara Kebira arranged for the publication of a volume of Biblical commentaries and homilies authored over a period of more than a century, by a number of its learned ancestors. In 1972, a descendant of the same family published in Jerba a volume of Talmudic commentary written in the 18th century by one of his forebears, interspersed with a printed dialogue, in the form of a commentary, between this great-great-grandson and his learned ancestor. These two books, the occasion and form of their publication, illustrate some of the characteristic features of Jerban scholarship and religious style which have imbued them with such continuing vitality.

The earlier volume of Biblical commentaries is entitled *Kiryat Arba'* (City of Four) and it was given this unusual title because it has not one, but four authors. Its primary author is Rabbi Rahamim Houri, a learned figure in Hara Kebira who flourished in the late 18th and early 19th century. The other three are his son Menahem, his grandson Ishaq (d. 1868) and his great-grandsom Rahamim (d. 1892); the editor, Jacob Houri (d. 1928), represents yet an additional generation of direct descendants. Only the second Rabbi Rahamim actually served as a rabbi in the community. None of the others held any official religious position but earned their livelihood as merchants and craftsmen. The commentaries they created — some in a mystical spirit, others following a more literary interpretation of the Biblical text — grew out of their participation in morning and evening study groups and comparable voluntary activities. This four-layered commentary represents more than the continuity of an intellectual tradition within a single family. The printed version of these texts has erased the temporal boundaries between generations. On the printed page, Rabbi Rahamim of the 18th century and his great-grandson of one hundred years later can talk to each other.

The volume published in Jerba in 1972 is entitled *Kisei Rahamim* (The Seat of Rahamim) and is a collection of commentaries on the Talmudic tractate of *Berakhot* — a portion of the Talmud which is largely concerned with the rules governing prayers and blessings. Its author is the 18th century Rabbi Rahamim Houri and its editor and commentator, his direct descendant, Rabbi Houaitu Houri who served as a teacher in Hara Kebira and who died only a few years ago. In his introduction he explains how he came to edit and publish the volume:

Unpublished manuscript of a 19th century scholar.

I now decided that, since I was a teacher of the Torah to many students, I would devote my energy to the compilation and copying of the holy writings of the elder of our family, one of the original (scholars of Jerba), Rabbi Rahamim Houri the first, who lived in our city of Jerba approximately two hundred years ago. He left behind (writings) containing great blessings and approaches to the study of most portions of the Talmud. I accomplished this transcription in the free time at my disposal during the noon breaks and during the night-time hours. I also did this in the course of my actual teaching, studying these holy manuscripts with students. I benefited a great deal from these writings and suceeded in penetrating his (i.e. Rabbi Rahamim's) approach to studying the tractate of *Berakhot* which appears in the present book entitled *Kisei Rahamin*. I also included some selections from his writings on other tractates.

Neither time nor subject matter are the major organizing principles of this work. As a concluding supplement to the new edition of the commentary on the tractate of *Berakhot*, we find a series of short comments on an entirely different Talmudic volume, the tractate of *Hulin*. These were composed by the members of an evening study group in 1972, just prior to the new publication of the volume. Connecting the two diverse parts of the work is the fact that the study group met in the same upper chamber of the Houri family compound where the earlier Rabbis studied and taught. In the eyes of the Jerban Jews, it is the shared place and the shared activity which unite the volume — and which unite much else in the Jewish culture of Jerba.

First the shared place. It is, of course, the island of Jerba; specifically the two Jewish villages on the island. Jerba is "the antechamber of Jerusalem"; it is, in the view of some of its scholars, within the legal realm and orbit of the Holy Land. The shared activity is not only the study of the same texts and commentaries but also the creation of books which testify that Jerba remains, in the words of one of its rabbis: "a community of scholars, scribes and of mighty, renowned rabbis who have penetrated the depths of scripture and the very essence of religious law." By virtue of their claimed antiquity and special status, every event in its history, every controversy within the community assumes more than local significance and is worthy of being recorded, documented and fully discussed.

The communities have preserved no organized archives — even of their recent past. What they deemed worthy of preservation found its way into print and still continues to do so, and thus has become a kind of living, on-going archive. Biographies of rabbis, teachers or ancestors, charters of local charitable societies, stories of local miracles, exchanges of correspondence on current or past community issues all serve to legitimize the special position the Jerbans wish to assume.

These fragments of Jerban collective memory are dispersed as prologues, epilogues and marginalia in numerous Jerban books. By far the most ambitious and most important effort to bring these together is the four-volume compilation of Rabbi Moshe Khalfon Hacohen, entitled *Brith Kehuna* (*The Covenant of Priesthod*) published in Jerba between 1940 and 1962. The table of organization follows that of the *Shulhan 'Arukh* — the compendium of Jewish religious law compiled in the late 16th century and accepted as authoritative by Jews everywhere. What we have then is not a commentary, but a Jerban supplement to this classic compilation. And, indeed, the *Brith Kehuna* has in turn become a classic for Jerban Jews, and Rabbi Khalfon is considered by Jerbans as a latter day Maimonides.

In his introduction, Rabbi Khalfon asserts, that it is absolutely prohibited to tamper with the accumulated corpus of local customs and regulations decreed by Jerban rabbis of past generations and that, even when they are at variance with Jewish practice elsewhere, these have the full authority of rabbinic law. Since these customs and regulations had multiplied and were preserved only in the oral tradition, Rabbi Khalfon felt impelled to put them in writing as a handy reference for the community and its leaders. In the following pages Rabbi Khalfon discusses and elaborates more than 700 specifically Jerban Jewish practices covering virtually every aspect of private, public and religious life.

Some examples:

RAIN: It is an accepted custom here on the island of Jerba and its region that, if no rain has fallen by the 17th day of *Heshvan* (approximately, mid-November), the judges of the Rabbinic Court (*dayyanim*) announce the following in all synagogues on that Sabbath: All individuals who are able to should undertake three fast days on the succeeding Monday, Thursday and Monday.

If by the new moon of *Kislev* (approximately December 1st), still no rain has fallen, the Rabbinic Court (*beth din*) decrees three obligatory fast days for the entire community — namely the following Monday, Thursday and Monday. And this is to be proclaimed to the community on the Sabbath in all the synagogues.

RAIN: It is a custom here on the island of Jerba — may God oversee its protection — that in case of an absence of rainfall the community is to recite the Song of Songs on the holy Sabbath day, just before the Torah is removed from the Ark.

PALM TREES: The fermented sap of palm trees is called *lagmi tayyib*. People hereabouts are careful not to purchase it from Christians because of the suspicion of its admixture with non-kosher wine. It is reported on the authority of Rabbi Haim Cohen, the chief rabbi of Gafsa, that some Christians, in all innocence, mix wine with the sap of the palm tree in order to improve its taste. At the occasion when the grapes begin to ripen, people hereabouts are wary of purchasing this fermented beverage from any gentile — even from a Muslim, because of their experience that some of them mix it with sour grape juice in order to ferment it.

ZGUGU: Concerning the fruit which in Arabic is called *zququ* or *zgugu*, I have heard that at a certain celebration some of the early learned authorities here were in doubt about the appropriate blessing for it since they did not know whether it was the fruit of a tree or the fruit of the earth. Present among them was either my grandfather Rabbi Moshe Cohen or his son, my uncle, Rabbi David Cohen, and he told them that he had heard from his father that zgugu and those nuts which in Arabic are called *bunduq* or *lawz libayi* are of the same kind. The only difference between them is that one is grown in an orchard and one grows wild in the desert. It is for this reason that they pronounced on it the blessing of the fruit of the tree.

TEACHING: The system of teaching customary among the teachers of the Torah, here on the island of Jerba, is as follows. Any person who is capable of independent study of the Talmud, who is able to read the Biblical texts properly and able to translate and explain them in Arabic, shall have at his disposal one of the synagogues of the town in which to teach Torah. In that place he can receive the children who come to study the alphabet, the recitation of the Bible, and then its interpretation in Arabic (which is termed *sharh*), after which he can teach them Talmud. The children should be divided into groups — those studying the alphabet, those studying the simple text of the Bible, those studying the text and its interpretation in Arabic, those studying one or another of the tractates of the Talmud. In this manner each student absorbs a moral education from his rabbi from his childhood until he reaches manhood.

In this modest, patient and occasionally picturesque manner, Jerbans have translated that which they share with Jews elsewhere and have adapted it to their local context of a Jewish culture immersed in a Muslim environment. The printed word of Jerba is both an expression of and a stimulus to their particular localistic form of Judaism.

In a study of Jerban Jews who have emigrated to Israel, Shlomo Deshen has quite correctly characterized their continuing literary activity as a "ritualization of literacy"[1] and of intellectual life. In other words, it is not so much the content of a book that is important or that leads to its publication. To publish a book, to buy it and to have it in one's home are prophylactic acts. The book becomes equivalent to a talisman. But there is more to it than that. The politics of literary activity and the consistent, even fierce attachment to a specifically Jerban style of book learning and book production have played a central role in the ability of this community to resist disintegration during a period when all other Jewish communities of North Africa have disappeared. Furthermore, it is quite likely that the Jerban book still contributes to the maintenance of Jerban identity even at a distance of several thousand miles from the island and several decades after they have left it.

The inception and growth of publishing in Jerba at the beginning of this century expressed a policy of strengthening the indigenous cultural system against outside threats. It coincided with the community's unqualified rejection of western-inspired education, of French language and culture and of any outside control of their way of life. The efflorescence of publishing corresponded with a consolidation of the local tradition and of its modes of transmission and reproduction.

The coincidence of these two developments is probably not accidental. For the Jerban religious leadership, it was not merely a question of studying and mastering the corpus of traditional knowledge and of reinforcing religious observance, a preoccupation common to orthodox Jews the world over. Rather, these universal components of their religious life were subjected to a process of "Jerbanization," elaborated in accents and chants which were specifically Jerban. Simply to designate their religious attitude as orthodox or conservative or traditional would be inadequate. In its recent history, the Jerban community has demonstrated a continuing flexibility and creativity in blending its local concerns with the broader tradition of universal Judaism.

1.   S. DESHEN, "The Work of Tunisian Scholars in Israel," *American Ethnologist*, II, 1975, pp. 251–259.

6
Merchants and Craftsmen

The market: place of interaction between Jews and Muslims.

The weekly market of Mahboubine, a village on the southern portion of the island.

From Community to Market

No matter how intense their ritual and intellectual activities, Jerban Jews have, still, somehow to make a living. Indeed, no man in Jerba is a full citizen, able to fulfill his religious and communal responsibilities, without establishing himself as an independent craftsman or merchant.

In a recent in-depth study of the bazaar economy of Sefrou, Morocco, Clifford Geertz observes "that the leaders of the religious institution and (if we may call it that) the commercial institution are the same people, that the main locus of the orthodox Sunni community in Sefrou, the *ummah* in the strict sense of the term, is the bazaar."[1] What is true for the Muslim ummah of Sefrou is even truer for the Jewish *qahal* of Jerba. Not only the leaders of the community, but virtually all able-bodied adult males are involved as sellers, producers or financiers of the Jerban economy and marketplace. As in Sefrou, the Jewish artisans and merchants are coterminous with the qahal. The ties which connect the economic activities of Jerban Jews to the qahal — to the whole of their communal life and its perpetuation — are not identical with those Geertz observed in Sefrou. They are not explicit, formal or structured, but rather, implicit and unstated. Nevertheless, they are pervasive and omnipresent. The organic relationship between the way the Jerban Jews earn their livelihoods and their ability to maintain their traditional religious and social system has remained effective in the face of profound political and technological changes over the past century. That is, the form of their economic life is both an expression of their communal particularity and a reinforcement of it.

100

In the market place of Hara Kebira.

The marketplace is also the locus of the most frequent and varied contact between Jews and Muslims, and consequently is the arena in which important aspects of identity, self-image and mutual perceptions are defined and enacted. Although the ethnic and religious boundaries separating Muslims and Jews are by no means absent or obliterated in the market-place, it is here that the lines of demarcation are most fluid and permeable. There is no religious barrier to the exchange of goods and services between Jerban Jew and Jerban Muslim; the commercial practices and economic mores of the Jews are, on the whole, those of the traditional North African who works in the bazaar. Their conception of what economic life is all about, of how it should be conducted, is shared with Jerban Muslims and, indeed, with Muslims in North Africa generally. Yet the actual shape and arrangement which these notions and practices take on are very markedly affected by their Jewish identity.

The almost complete coincidence of the Jews in the market and the male Jews of the community is a fairly recent configuration. Up until about 1910, the structure of Jerban Jewish economic life was quite different in several respects. Then, as now, the Jews were in the market, but, unlike recent times when the Jews have been prominent in only a few discrete areas, the Jews in the 18th and 19th centuries controlled most sectors of the permanent market at Houmt Souk. Older Jewish stall owners recall the times when the *suq al-arba'a* — the covered portion of Houmt Souk's market — was so completely deserted on a Saturday that one could play soccer undisturbed along its empty alleyways. Jewish economic activity at that time extended beyond the *suq* to the dispersed Muslim hamlets and estates which dotted the Jerban countryside — the so-called *ghaba*, — and even beyond the island to the towns and oases of south Tunisia and Tripolitania.

101

H

In spite of its severe contraction during the past five or six decades, both in numbers and in scope, the Jewish participation in the economic life of the island has exhibited some fundamental qualitative continuities. Jews occupied and continue to occupy an ecological niche in the chain of Jerban economic life. Their presence or absence in certain fields of commerce, services or craftsmanship was not random. The distribution of Jews in the occupational structure of the island did not correspond to that of the Muslim population, but derived from a kind of ethnic division of labor. In those occupations and pursuits in which they were represented, Jews tended to be very active. Some occupations such as jewelry, carpentry and tailoring were almost exclusively Jewish. In others, such as blacksmithing, petty commerce or the grocery trade, they were represented in significant numbers, sharing the market for these services with Muslim counterparts.

In certain sectors, they were completely absent. There were no Jews in agriculture. Jews had virtually no role in the cultivation of the island's major crops such as dates, olives and cereals, nor in the production of olive oil, nor in the local distribution of these agricultural commodities — although Jews were of considerable importance in their distribution on the wholesale and export level. Fishing, like agriculture, was devoid of Jewish participation. Some Jews reportedly dealt with dried fish and, very briefly, with the canning of the tuna catch. Raising of livestock (mostly sheep) was another activity from which Jews were almost entirely absent, as they were from the thriving pottery industry of the southern part of the island. No prohibition prevented Jews from engaging in certain pursuits nor did any official enactments push them to concentrate in others. There is a simple but compelling reason for this spontaneous division. Economic activity was embedded in a system of social relations which were, in large measure, determined by one's ethnic or religious affiliation. The pursuits of a living and of fulfilling God's commandments overlapped. Community and marketplace touched at many points.

Neither the process of entering the marketplace nor the economic and other relationships between its Jewish participants, nor the nature and limits of their interaction with non-Jews can be understood without taking into consideration their communal aspect. The local textile industry is a perfect case in point.

A Jerban proverb says that "the life of Jerba's inhabitants hangs by a thread." This refers to the wool for textile weaving which was one of the island's chief industries. The manufacture of wool textiles, especially the renowned Jerban blankets which were exported all over the Mediterranean, absorbed a great part of its productive energies. The traditional cycle of production of wool and textiles provides an instructive illustration of the irregular pattern of Muslim-Jewish division of labor. Sheep are raised only by Muslims. Wool from the sheep raised on Jerba is supplemented by large quantities imported from the continent. Jewish entrepreneurs — especially from Hara Sghira — played an important role in the wholesale commerce of raw wool and in the carding process. Spinning the wool was virtually the exclusive prerogative of the Muslim women of the island and, more interestingly, weaving was an entirely Muslim male occupation. As far as we know no Jews were involved in this stage of the production of wool textiles. This is a curious kind of division of labor since, in former times, many of the weaving ateliers (nul), whose architecturally distinctive shapes dot the Jerban landscape, were manned by Muslim weavers working for Jewish entrepreneurs on a commission basis. In sharp contrast, dyeing, the next process in the production of textiles, was a craft entirely in Jewish hands. At the beginning of this century, it was one of the two main occupations (the other being jewelry) of Jerban Jews. Their vats and their workshops were located in Houmt Souk to which the dyers commuted daily from their homes in Hara Kebira. In 1979, there was only one Jewish dyer left in Houmt Souk, the only one who still fired his dyeing vats in the traditional manner with the seasoned trunks of olive trees. Technological changes and Jewish emigration have resulted in the near disappearance of this traditional craft.

Jews played a major, even dominant, role in the trade in woollen textiles. In the early years of this century, the special market for woollen blankets was held in Houmt Souk every Wednesday. So prominent was the role of Jewish entrepreneurs in this commerce that, if a major Jewish festival fell on a Wednesday, the market in this commodity was paralyzed and no business whatsoever was transacted.

It is indeed difficult in this particular case to discern any regular or structural pattern in the division of tasks between Jews and Muslims at the different stages in production of woolen textiles. The distribution of economic roles followed a zigzag and irregular line. Within this configuration, three features seem to be constant. First, and most important, one can observe an occupational concentration buttressed by social ties and an ethnic network. At whichever points on the continuum of wool processing, textile production and distribution Jews or Muslims were active, they were active in some numbers but not necessarily as a group. Second, Jews tended in this particular case to predominate in the entrepreneurial and distributive activities connected with the textile industry. This was not necessarily true of many other occupations. Third, the relationships among Jews themselves, or between Jews and Muslims were never those of employer and employee, but rather associative in nature, consisting of commissions, partnerships of various kinds and specific agreements for discrete transactions.

Going Out to the Ghaba

The traditional code of honor recognized and accepted throughout Muslim North Africa implied complete social segregation between men and women. Except for husbands and close family, contacts with women, conversation with women, even the sight of women was prohibited and prevented. All social, economic and cultural institutions adjusted to this reality. Because of their inferior status in the eyes of North African Muslims, only Jews and Blacks were, to some extent, exempt from this taboo. In the case of the Jews, this partial exemption led, in many parts of North Africa, to their concentration in trades and professions which by their very nature involved contact with Muslim women or entry into the precincts of the household. In rural areas and among semi-nomadic groups this meant that most of the itinerant merchants and craftsmen — that is, peddlers, tinkers and tailors — were Jews. This was true for southern Tunisia and, most particularly, for the island of Jerba itself where until recently, when modern means of transportation and a changed system of distribution eliminated the need for their services, all the peddlers and itinerants were Jews from the two Haras.

Among the Jews (and the Muslims) this system was known as "going out to the *ghaba*" — literally the forest. All itinerant occupations are included by this phrase. In practical terms, going out to the ghaba meant wandering from one *menzel* to another and travelling to hamlets and villages of the island and of the southern part of the country.

The following are descriptions by former residents of Jerba who observed the system in their youth and whose parents spent years wandering through the ghaba:

> ...In spite of the numerous professions in which the Jews of Jerba were engaged, they did not find it easy to earn their livelihood. Many had no choice but to leave their homes and wander as peddlers to Arab settlements in distant places, at the risk of great personal danger, not to speak of the great suffering, hunger and thirst caused by constant movement from place to place. They would travel as far as the Libyan desert, and to the localities around the towns of Medenine, Tatahouine, Jabal al-Hwayya, Matmata, etc. Some would travel between the bedouin encampments for the three-month period of the summer, which coincided with the harvests, when the nomads had ready cash available. Some of these itinerant merchants would return home to Jerba just in time for the High Holidays in the early fall, laden with the fruit of their labors acquired through much toil and at great personal risk.[2]

The author of this passage goes on to reminisce about his own father, a jeweler from Hara Kebira, who specialized in the production of a certain item of jewelry for which there was a great demand in the distant Arab settlements. After spending the entire summer travelling to the villages and encampments on the continent, he would return to Jerba in early September just prior to the fall cycle of Jewish festivals. On one such occasion, when he was travelling alone through the desert on the way to Jerba, he was set upon by an armed bandit who was about to rob him of his entire season's profits and thus leave him and his family destitute. Miraculously, in answer to his prayers, the disembodied voice of some invisible being sent the bandit scurrying in fear and saved the jeweler's life and fortune.

Such miraculous encounters with strange spirits and beings are a frequent theme of Jerban Jewish folktales. However, by all accounts, acts of banditry and violence against itinerant Jewish craftsmen and merchants were quite rare. Although they are not mentioned in any of our sources, it is very likely that these peddlers enjoyed formal and informal arrangements of protection and clientage with the various groups among whom they worked. The comparative security of their travels in these sparsely policed areas is strong testimony to the importance and value which the Arab villagers and tribesmen of the region attached to the services provided by the Jewish peddlers. There were certainly many precarious aspects of their existence. Some they shared with all the inhabitants of the region and some resulted from the fact of their being Jews. However, the niche that they filled in the regional ecology and the relationships with their Muslim neighbors that this supposed and generated, made them not only a necessary but even a welcome component of the tribal and ethnic mosaic of Southern Tunisia.

The Jewish peddler, mounted on his mule or donkey, has slowly disappeared from the landscape. Jerban Jewish participation in trans-Saharan trade, of which there is some mention in mid-19th century sources, has ceased entirely. By the turn of the century, instead of sending out seasonal peddlers, the two Jewish communities of Jerba exported groups of permanent settlers — craftsmen and traders — to the villages and towns of southern Tunisia such as Zarzis, Medenine, Tatahouine and Ben Gardane, whose Jewish communites were formed almost wholly by migrants from Jerba. This network of permanent settlements, with their jewellers, tailors and petty entrepreneurs was a miniature replica of the mother community. They provided, on a more regular and sedentary basis, the services for the surrounding Muslim population which had previously been rendered by itinerant craftsmen and peddlers. An equally, if not more, important consequence of the proliferation of these permanent settlements was the creation of a Jewish archipelago in southern Tunisia whose religious and intellectual capital was Jerba. The jurisdiction of the rabbinical court of Jerba prevailed from Sfax southward to the Libyan border.

In terms of the number of people involved and its impact on the community, the system of itinerant peddling confined to the island itself was of far greater importance than were the seasonal excursions to the continent. The classic ghaba system was one which involved only Jerbans — both Jews and Muslims.

The peddlers would take a knapsack containing needles, combs, odorific spices and textiles and wander to the Arab villages exchanging these commodities for wheat, barley, beans, eggs, millet, old clothes, etc. The Jewish peddler would be subject to all sorts of insults and humiliations and was the target of stones thrown by children. He suffered all of this in order to earn his crust of bread. Those (peddlers) travelled to the (Arab) villages to sew clothes or woollen garments or to plate copper utensils or to purchase fruits and vegetables. They sometimes bought the entire harvest of a garden or orchard and would go to collect some of the produce each day. These people would rise at dawn, perform their morning prayers either in the synagogue, or, if they had to travel some distance, in their homes. They would then mount their donkeys to bring back their merchandise, or they would set out on foot and return in the evening or even after nightfall.[3]

Concerning Jewish carpenters, another Jerban author tells us:

> Some of the menfolk would seek work in the Arab villages (e.g. carpenters). They leave the Hara on Sunday and return on Thrusday evening. Customarily, they did not do any heavy work on Fridays.[4]

Viewed from a broad perspective, the ghaba system was a rather bold extension of the structural pattern described earlier, which divided the daily, weekly or seasonal rhythm of Jerban Jewish lives between home and market, between holy and profane. Those who earned their livelihood from itinerant work, severed from their communal setting for days or weeks on end, found themselves in prolonged and unmediated contact with Muslims with whom they could share neither food nor religious rituals, but with whom they did share a great number of cultural traits. It is not surprising, therefore, that the relationships which regulated their interaction went beyond a simple unadorned exchange of goods and services.

The quality, character and extent of such relationships in their Jerban, North African setting are illustrated by the case of the *delwaji*, who practiced the now extinct craft of producing irrigation buckets. His craft was not simply a matter of producing and selling but involved long-term, sometimes even multi-generational relationships.

> The buckets for drawing water were made of leather. They were wide on the top and narrow on the bottom. They were produced by Jews, and only the Jews were masters of this craft. These Jewish craftsmen were tied to their Arab customers for the entire year in order to maintain and repair the bucket for them. Each Jewish bucket-maker had a customary claim on the work for a particular Arab, one which passed from father to son. As compensation for his service, the Jewish craftsman was a kind of partner in the Arab's agricultural activity and received a certain percentage of the yield from him. At each season, the Arab would deliver this share to the very home of the Jew — be it a measure of millet, or dates or barley or fruit. The Jew would in turn take the produce to be sold in the market of the Hara.
> The Jewish bucket-maker usually maintained such ties with more than one Arab. Even in the hottest days of the summer, he would travel to their estates and repair whatever was needed. The same type of relationship still obtains with respect to black servants who are the exclusive practitioners of the craft of barbering. These shave and barber entire families all year round. Since the extended Arab family sometimes comprehends as many as 50 souls — field workers, servants, etc. — the black servant shaves them all and receives his wage in the harvest season in the form of dates, barley, etc.[5]

This text provides us with a fascinating glimpse of the workings of a system of non-monetary exchange in its economic and social aspects. There were no salaries. Labor and services were paid for in kind, with products which could either be offered for sale on the market or consumed by one's family. To work was to assure one's own survival and that of one's family rather than to accumulate profit. Personal ties and not an employer-employee nexus connected the parties in an exchange. The definition and reproduction of each person's status was dependent to a greater extent on ethnic or religious affiliation than on a specific occupation. Also, a very special ethic prevailed. Even during the heat of the summer, the Jewish delwaji did not default on his obligation, just as the Arab peasant did not fail to "deliver to the very doorstep of the Jew his share of the harvest." We shall see some surviving manifestations of this ethic among the jewelers of Hara Kebira.

Besides the tailors, peddlers, bucket-makers and handymen of all sorts, there were also others who ventured forth into the countryside. There were the carpenters of Hara Sghira who carried their tools with them, the harness-makers and the jewelers. Even some women took their skills to the ghaba, offering their services as seamstresses and embroiderers or selling cloth and notions and carrying back, in return, the produce of the countryside. Unlike the males, however, they stayed away from the Hara only for the day. In a word, all occupations which were to be found in a sedentary form in the Hara or in Houmt Souk were also represented in an itinerant form in the ghaba. The ghaba was an extension of the permanent market. There was no particular stigma attached to itinerant activity. All types of families and all types of individuals were represented, including some of the most respected and most learned rabbis of the community. We do not have complete information concerning the details of exchange and compensation between these various types of itinerant crafts-men and their Muslim customers in the ghaba. They were probably not identical with those of the delwaji as described above. However, they almost certainly incorporated the same qualitative features which characterized, and still characterize, economic exchange among Jerbans.

These itinerant economic relationships were neither anarchic nor random. On the level of the community, there existed an informal but recognized and effective division of the island between the two communities of Hara Kebira and Hara Sghira. For example, the southern portion of the island was the domain of the latter, while the central and northern portions were the domain of the former. The itinerants of one town did not frequent the villages and hamlets reserved for the itinerants of the other. On the individual level, peddlers and crafts-men did not simply wander around knocking on strange doors hoping to find work or trade. Each had his own territory, his own group of estates among which he circulated from Sunday through Thursday. The Muslims with whom he traded or whom he serviced were not properly speaking customers, but were clients, previously known to him or with whom he, or his family, had an ongoing connection of exchange and credit and possibly even protection.

The ghaba system continued to provide a livelihood for a significant number of Jerban Jews as late as the 20's and 30's of this century. It was the victim of a transportation revolu-tion on the island, and today the Jewish peddler has become an anachronism. Only dispersed symbolic remnants of the once widespread form of commerce survive. A donkey dealer from Hara Kebira still travels about the island and the adjacent continental areas buying and selling donkeys and mules. A small number of jewelers, tailors and wool-dealers travel to the weekly markets to take orders, to deliver goods and to maintain contact with their customers and clients in the outlying areas. A few elderly Jewish money-lenders, some of them former peddlers themselves, make the rounds of the weekly markets in order to collect debts or explore new opportunities for small investments. Except for two professions, the periodic markets have replaced the homestead as a meeting place. The few remaining mattress makers from Hara Kebira and the rather numerous carpenters from Hara Sghira continue to travel to the individual menzels and building sites.

Communal Contraction and Economic Expansion

Between the first years of this century and the present day, the occupational distribution of Jerban Jews has — as one would expect — changed considerably. Demographic developments (fewer Jews and more Muslims), and political and technological changes have had their cumulative effect. Nonetheless the new boundaries which these shifts created continue to preserve their economic niche and to form part of a larger pattern which serves to maintain their cultural identity and communal autonomy.

A comparison between the data from the Tunisian Archives of 1902 based on a sample of 183 male Jews of Hara Kebira and an informal but comprehensive survey of the Hara in 1977-78 demonstrates both the shifts and the continuity in their occupational distribution.

The figures for 1902 are incomplete since there were almost certainly more than 183 economically active males in Hara Kebira at that time. If rigorous quantitative comparisons with the current situation are thus excluded, significant trends and qualitative changes are quite discernible. Certain archaic trades like that of the delwaji (bucketmaker) or the *tanakji* (coffeepot makers) disappeared, but other more modern occupations such as watch-maker and those connected with automobiles have made their appearance. In several areas, one observes a rather dramatic diminution of Jewish participation, especially in general commerce (from 47 in 1902 to 14 in 1977-78) and in the wholesale and retail distribution of foodstuffs (26 in 1902 to 11 in 1977-78). Jewish merchants did not, apparently, withstand the movement toward compulsory cooperatives instigated by the government policies of Ben Salah during the 1960's. The caravanserais, food depots and textile stores once belonging to the Jews are today either deserted or have changed hands.

Occupation	1902	1977-1978
Commerce	47	14
Jewelers	28	120
Food sellers (miscellaneous)	19	6
Tailors	13	24
Grocers	9	3
Cobblers	8	2
Butchers	6	2
Brokers	6	0
Tinsmiths	6	0
Schoolteachers	6	9
Blacksmiths	5	4
Carpenters	5	1
Millers	5	0
Masons, builders	5	2
Embroiderers	4	0
Cooks, makers of *briks*	3	3
Dyers	3	5
Carders (wool)	2	0
Makers of coffee pots	2	0
Tobacco sellers	1	0
Bucketmakers (*delwaji*)	1	0
Scribes	1	2
Auto repairs, tires	0	5
Watchmakers	0	5
Drivers	0	1
Insurance	0	1
Mattress makers	0	3
Coachmen	0	1
Moneylenders	0	8

From the beginning of this century, the Jews of Jerba did not branch out into any new trades in significant numbers. There were no new professional departures; watchmaking, which was not practiced in 1902, is a variation of the jewelry trade, and the manual trades connected with automobile maintenance and repair are an extension of the traditional Jerban Jewish occupation of blacksmithing. In this regard, it is most striking that not a single Jew who remained in Jerba entered any of the liberal professions or any branch of the greatly expanded state bureaucratic sector (e.g., no post office, municipal or bank employees). Nor did any embark upon a career connected with the growth of numerous modern technologies and services. On the contrary, and most significantly, we observe a greater concentration of Jerban Jews in fewer fields of economic endeavor. The response to their reduced numbers and to the emergence of new circumstances which might threaten their livelihood and their communal existence was to withdraw into fewer trades and cluster in them in larger numbers. They thus concentrated their economic relations in occupations which had secure internal lines of communication and which moved along networks that were almost totally within the boundaries of the community. The social and other inter-actions between Jerban Jews and their non-Jewish neighbors did not necessarily undergo any qualitative change as a result of this shift. Rather, the economic space occupied by the Jews contracted while its internal density increased.

In a sense, the coincidence of market and community has, in recent times, become much more pronounced than in earlier periods and the patterns of economic life have become more obviously intertwined with the various processes of social integration and cultural reproduction of the community. Indeed, the internal structure of Jewish artisanal and com-mercial activity derives its rationale less from the exigencies of the marketplace than from the paradigms and needs of their community. An examination of the jewelry trade — which is by far the dominant occupation of males in the Hara, and whose quantitative importance is still increasing — illustrates this relationship between community and economy.

The Gold Rush

In absolute figures, the number of Jewish jewelers has remained the same since the beginning of the century. Although the incomplete survey of 1902 counts only 28 jewelers, Victor Fleury, the author of a more complete inventory, speaks of "40 workshops employing 120 men and 30 children."[6] Our 1978 survey shows a total of 120 jewelers at all stages of their careers. When considered in the context of the villages' radically reduced Jewish population, this shows a remarkable growth. Approximately 15% of the total Jewish population of Hara Kebira is engaged in one or another aspect of jewelry production, and of the economically active male population of the Hara (i.e., those who are 14 years and older) the percentage is approximately 50% and is growing. At the present time there is scarcely a household in the Hara which does not contain one or more jewelers among its members. As many as 80% of the young men entering the labor market after their yeshiva studies have chosen careers in the jewelry profession (most of the remaining 20% opt for tailoring).

The movement toward jewelry is sweeping aside all other traditional career choices and includes men who have trained for, or even practiced other crafts. It has overturned earlier patterns of inherited occupations. A few examples will suffice to show how powerful this movement is. In one branch of the Sebagh family, the great-grandfather was the Jerban-born rabbi of Medenine; the grandfather was a very prosperous religious scribe who earned his living from writing Torahs, phylacteries and *mezuzot*; the father served for many years as one of the community's ritual slaughterers and as a *wakil*, a kind of para-legal expert, who advised residents of the Hara when they had cases pending before the local rabbinic court. The three sons of this man, now ranging in age from 22 to 32 years, all received a thorough grounding in traditional learning. Nonetheless, all are now practicing jewelers, each with his own separate stall in Houmt Souk.

Or take the case of the Soufir family. The great-grandfather, Ouzifa, was a peddler in the ghaba. His two sons continued this trade, combining it with petty commerce in Houmt Souk. Of the eight sons of these two brothers, only four are still left in Jerba. All of them, now in their forties and fifties, are prosperous jewelers in the Hara and Houmt Souk. Their grown sons (over 15 years old), now numbering ten, are all jewelers with their own stalls in the suq or workshops in the Hara. All fourteen of Ouzifa's economically active descendants are engaged in one phase or another of the jeweler's trade. Those who are still

The senior member of a family of three generations of jewellers in his stall in Houmt Souk.
The oldest and most respected jewellers in the market.

minors will undoubtedly follow the same route. Not a single one of Ouzifa's male descendants still residing in Jerba has opted for any other profession.

A slightly different pattern is exemplified by another family. The father, now in his sixties, gained his livelihood until recently as a bicycle repairer. Rather late in life, he switched professions, taking up jewelry not as a seller, but as a specialized producer of the large silver ankle bracelets (*khalkhal*) which are *de rigueur* at every traditional Tunisian wedding. He is one of three Jewish jewelers in Jerba who specialize almost exclusively in the production of this particular piece of jewelry. His oldest son was trained as a tailor and was the proprietor of a successful tailoring establishment in Houmt Souk. So powerful was the pull of the jewelry business — and so promising did its opportunities appear — that he converted half of his tailor shop into a jewelry store and workshop. The youngest son of the family, who was trained as a television mechanic, abandoned this calling to specialize in the production of heavy gold bracelets. Settled in Marseilles, a third son is also a jeweler. The same inexorable trend toward jewelry can, with slight variations, be documented in numerous other households of Hara Kebira.

As the number of jewelers increases, so naturally does the space this trade occupies. The large stalls in the traditional jeweler's market in Houmt Souk are being subdivided to accommodate the influx of new craftsmen. Shops are constantly being added and its boundaries now extend into new areas of the marketplace. In the Hara itself, this spatial expansion is even more dramatic. The number of workshops and even of small factories has multiplied and, for the first time, a number of retail jewelry shops have made their appearance. Hara Sghira, previously immune, has also been affected by this proliferation. There are now three jewelers' stalls in that village.

Why this gold rush? Of all the occupations Jerban Jews traditionally practiced, that of jewelry was least affected by the momentous changes which have overtaken Tunisian society in the past century. The demand among the Muslim population of southern Tunisia for hand-made jewelry of traditional design has not abated over the years. A threefold growth in the region's population, a sustained period of general prosperity and the infusion of funds repatriated from the menfolk working abroad have fueled an increased demand. At the same time, the cultural factors which require the presentation of jewelry to one's womenfolk on the occasion of marriages or annual feasts remained unchanged. In 1979, a Jerban jeweler estimated that the family of an average middle class Muslim groom spent between 750 to 1500 Tunisian dinars ($1875-3750) on jewelry for the bride. The figure often reached several times these sums. During the past several decades gold has replaced silver as the universally preferred metal for women's ornaments. This further augmented the demand for new jewelry by requiring the substitution of gold for the hereditary silver objects accumulated over many generations.

Jerban Jews do not lack for work. The departure of large numbers of Jewish jewelers from Jerba and other parts of Tunisia, has left a much smaller pool of artisans among whom this increased demand is distributed. The geographical radius of the demand for Jerban production has extended beyond southern Tunisia and now includes areas of the Sahel and even the region of Tunis itself. Given this extraordinary combination of circumstances, one can understand the unprecedented prominence of the jeweler's profession among Jerban Jews. In spite of various official efforts to encourage the entry of local Muslims into this occupation, very few have in fact joined its ranks. This is a puzzle. But here again, the effective organization of its work on an ethnic basis has, so far, posed an obstacle to any such intrusion.

Economic Activity
and Social Integration

The significant unit in the jewelry business in Jerba is not the family, not the company, not the firm, but the individual jeweler. Tracing the career of a Jerban jeweler is not simply to describe the different stages of his professional development and economic activity. It is also to plot the successive phases of his social and communal integration. This twofold process is one which, on both a professional and social level, leads from dependence to independence. Socially one moves along a continuum connecting the status of minor and yeshiva student to that of a full-fledged citizen in the community, capable of fulfilling all adult roles. Professionally, one begins the itinerary as an apprentice and culminates it as a retail merchant of jewelry. There are a number of intermediate stages in this career pattern: serving as an assistant to a master artisan, achieving independent status as a craftsman-producer, or combining production with retail selling. Spatially, this process leads the jeweler from the homogeneous Hara to the heterogeneous market, the place of contact with non-Jews.

Not every aspiring jeweler passes through all of these stages; only a few end up exclusively as merchants. But virtually every jeweler by his early 20's achieves the status of independent producer or that of an associate to an independent producer. Being someone's employee is not socially congenial nor is it a widespread phenomenon. This bias has many historical and geographical parallels in the context of Islamic North Africa and possibly even the Islamic world generally. Among the young men approaching their 20's, only the very poor, backward or unskilled remain employees.

The dominant modes and aspirations are either complete independence, or some form of association or partnership. While these forms of association do not necessarily imply any economic equality between the associates, they are all based on the notion of a minimal independent status of all parties. The various modes of association are sufficiently flexible to accommodate individuals representing an entire range of financial means. By his mid-20's every jeweler is on his own, and it is at this moment, also, that he enters the ranks of marriageable males. Economic independence is a prerequisite for finding a mate. By allowing males to become heads of families and full citizens, occupational maturation ties directly into the process of the reproduction of the community. In purely economic terms, there are no barriers to the creation of larger units of production which by utilizing paid workers would assure control of a large part of the market. Neither the capital nor the enterprising spirit required for such a project are lacking. But an innovation of this kind would shatter the social organization of the community, a result no one has an interest in bringing about.

Even though the economic distance (in terms of wealth) between the lowest level of professional independence and the highest point may be considerable, the social distance is not very great. Professional relationships between the jewelers are multiple — between specialists and generalists, between producers and sellers — with each category constantly dependent upon the other for work, products and services. Credit relationships between jewelers are complex and constantly shifting. This professional interaction supplements earlier ties of kinship, studentship, and the like. And just as the relationships between jewelers are multiple and multi-layered, so too does the individual jeweler fulfill several functions in different spheres simultaneously. A Jewish jeweler is not simply a jeweler; he may also be the head of a synagogue, a part-time scribe, the community circumciser, or a member of the burial society. In Jerba, possessing the skills to produce or sell jewelry is not enough to make one a jeweler. One has, first and foremost, to find a place within a closely knit social — even more than economic — network. Since similar rules govern other occupations, it is, once again, according to ethnic, religious and communal affiliations that the division of labor operates and perpetuates itself.

Ma'tuq the Jeweler

Ma'tuq is just under forty years old. He is the only son of a father who was a petty trader in Houmt Souk. Like virtually all the Jewish males of his age from the Hara, his education was exclusively within the framework of the traditional system of the yeshiva in which he continued as a full time student until the age of 15. From the time he was about 12, he would hang around the workshops of the jewelers in the Hara during his free time, observing their work, and helping them in small tasks. In this way, he began to learn the trade. At age 15, he left school and apprenticed himself to an established jeweler in Houmt Souk. He did not pay for his training, nor was he paid for his work during the period. As Ma'tuq puts it: his master profited from his work while he himself profited by learning the craft and gaining experience in the trade.

At 17, Ma'tuq left his master or, as the local usage has it, he liberated himself from his master and established an independent workshop in his home in the Hara. Here he began to produce jewelry for sale to the merchants who had stalls in Houmt Souk. Then (the early 1960's), as now, setting up an independent workshop did not require a large investment of capital. The basic tools and equipment for a workshop were simple and few. They included a working surface, a lamp or other source of light, a small torch and bottled gas, pliers, hammer, scissors and tweezers, many small containers, various chemicals for cleaning and bonding metals, a board with calibrated holes for making wire of different diameters, a scale, a melting pot and a vise. More recently, a large portrait of President Bourguiba and a radio with a cassette player have become indispensable requirements of every workshop. In the summer of 1979, a jeweler from the Hara estimated the cost of all items required to begin work on one's own as 60 to 100 dinars ($150–$200). When Ma'tuq began his independent career twenty years ago, he needed even less.

After only one year in his own workshop, he made the move from the Hara to Houmt Souk. He rented a small stall in the jeweler's market where he continued to make objects and to sell his own wares and those of others directly to Muslim customers. In the course of time, his enterprise prospered, he acquired a substantial clientele, and the structure of his activity was transformed. Today, he no longer manufactures objects. His manual efforts are now specialized and restricted to "finishing," that is to say, polishing and preparing the manufactured jewelry for display and sale. An increasing portion of his time is devoted to selling jewelry and to maintaining and expanding his network of clients. With his surplus capital, Ma'tuq finances the production, on a relatively large scale, of a certain type of decorated gold bracelet for which there exists a steady demand. He has thus become the supplier of this standard item of female Muslim ornamentation to most other merchants in the jeweler's market, supplementing his primarily retail role with that of a wholesaler.

Ma'tuq's professional progress from apprentice to retailer-wholesaler was parallelled by his social and cultural advancement. Soon after consolidating his professional independence by acquiring a stall in Houmt Souk, he married and established his own family. His move from the Hara was accompanied by a transformation of cultural habits which was characteristic of most of his male peers. He shed the traditional Jewish garb (baggy trousers, chechia, etc.) in favor of standard western clothing. Instead of working while seated on the floor or ground, he now works at a bench and table. Similar changes in life style have also infiltrated the domestic sphere. It is no longer at ground level that one eats, cooks and sleeps. As Jerbans straightened their bodies, they also raised their standard of living.

Ma'tuq's biography represents a paradigmatic case of the career of a Jerban Jewish jeweler. Yet many variations of the pattern it traces are possible. Facing Ma'tuq's stall is a much smaller shop belonging to Houaita, a jeweler some 17 years Ma'tuq's senior. The son of a respected rabbi and the descendant of a line of scholars and community leaders, Houaita was also apprenticed as a jeweler in his mid-teens. But this was in the early 1940's when economic opportunities for jewelers were neither as promising nor as abundant as they became several decades later. Instead of continuing as a jeweler, he opened a small drygoods store with capital provided by two well-to-do merchants. He shared his profits with them in a partnership-type arrangement known by its Aramaic name - 'isqa. According to this contract (a close relative of the Muslim qirad and medieval European commenda), one side furnishes most of the capital and the other all of the work and management while profits and losses are shared on an agreed-upon basis.

While he remains a layman, Houaita nevertheless maintains a high level of religious and communal involvement. He coordinates the affairs of the family synagogue, one of the most active in the community. He attends several weekly study groups, and is both an expert on and staunch supporter of local Jerban Jewish customs. He is the head of the Jewish burial society and, most importantly, has served for the past few decades as the circumciser for the community, a service which he provides gratis because it is a mitzva – a good deed.

The late 1960's was a difficult period for fetty commerce, which was placed under strong state supervision. At that time Houaita paid off his loan, abandoned his drygoods business and opened a small jewelry store. Not having practiced this craft for more than twenty years, he was not much of a jeweler, and his shop is a rather modest one. Manually, he does little more than repair chains, assemble necklaces and the like. His speciality is a certain type of necklace, the production of which he finances on a small scale and which, in addition to selling in his own stall, he also provides on a wholesale basis to others in Houmt Souk.

The considerable respect which he enjoys in the community bears no direct relationship to his rather limited wealth or economic power. Houaita's income is derived almost entirely from the sale of objects produced in the workshops of the Hara, including those belonging to his two jeweler sons — one aged 18 and the other 24. Both are economically independent of their father. The younger of the two has a thriving workshop in his father's house in the Hara, employing three apprentices. Here he produces a variety of jewelry, but specializes in a certain type of ring. The older son owns a stall in Houmt Souk not far from that of his father, but one with a much larger volume of business. From the point of view of craftsmanship and wealth, both sons are more successful than their father. When the latter needs stock for his stall, he buys it from his sons as he would from any other jeweler. At any given moment the credit balance between Houaita and his sons may amount to hundreds or even thousands of dinars. The same holds true for the exchange between the two brothers, highlighting the fact that among the Jews of Hara Kebira, kinship ties do not necessarily imply privileged economic ties. The separation of these two categories of relationship enables the sons of a family to acquire the economic independence which, as we indicated above, is a prerequisite for their full citizenship in the community.

This pattern is not universal. In Hara Sghira, for example, family enterprises, especially in carpentry, are the more common pattern. In some families in Hara Kebira, the pater familias retains absolute control of the family's economic resources, including the enterprises of all his sons. This, however, is exceptional. A young man seeks, and virtually always achieves, independence or some form of association or partnership with a colleague which is functionally equivalent to independence.

Qarus, the jeweller occupying the stall right next to Ma'tuq's, is now in his mid-twenties. His father is a custodian at the yeshiva and supplements his meager income by baking and selling pastries every Friday just before the Sabbath. His older brother is a tailor, married, and the father of a young and growing family. The family possesses very modest resources. Consequently, when Qarus concluded his apprenticeship and wished to establish himself in Houmt Souk, he lacked sufficient capital to acquire a stall, merchandise and other necessary furnishings. He was, however, in possession of a very valuable asset — a reputation as an able and enterprising craftsman.

People with means were willing to take a chance on him. Ma'tuq and another jeweler advanced the necessary capital (approximately 2,000 dinars at the time) on the condition that all of Qarus' profits, after expenses, would be divided equally between him and his backers. Put somewhat differently, Qarus would do all the work, his backers would provide him with the capital necessary to start his business and, in return, each would share equally in the risks and the profits. This arrangement, known by its Talmudic designation of 'isqa was, as we know from the documents of the Cairo Geniza, practiced by Tunisian and Egyptian Jewish merchants in the middle ages. In Jerba today, it continues to be the most prevalent form of partnership, not only between jewelers, but between Jewish craftsmen and merchants generally. Even though Qarus has owned his own stall for more than a decade now, and even though his capital worth has increased many times over his original investment, he continues to maintain this relationship with Ma'tuq.

Ma'tuq, in turn, is himself involved in a comprehensive partnership with one of the most successful jewelers in the suq. They share equally in the profits and risks of all their ventures. This latter jeweler is the epitome of a pure merchant jeweler. There is nothing random about his commerce. His stall in Houmt Souk is bare. It offers no display of tempting gold and silver ornaments. This is not a place for the casual browser and occasional customer. He no longer produces any jewelry himself, but has it produced by others exclusively for customers who order it from him. The only transactions which take place in his shop are the receipt of such orders and the subsequent delivery of the finished product. This pure transactional activity is made possible by his reputation for skill and his many years of reliable activity which have won him a large clientele on the island of Jerba and its environs.

Just like his Muslim Jerban neighbor, the Jerban Jewish jeweler is — even in his behavior in the market place — not a purely "economic man." His economic ties are interwined with his social ties and, in the case of a Jew, with his ethnic and religious identity. The form and extent of the strictly commercial relationships between the four jewelers upon whose careers we briefly touched — creditor, debtor, partners, associate — are inconceivable if removed from their social and ethnic setting. The same holds true for the intricate web of connections, deals and transactions among all the jewelers active in Houmt Souk.

Collaboration and Competition

The close connection between commerce and community does not exclude competition; on the contrary, it induces it. In the summer of 1979, there were 55 jewelry shops belonging to Jews in Houmt Souk. Of these, 42 are concentrated within the rather modest confines of the *suq al-sagha* — the *centre des bijoux.* Four are in the adjoining covered market, traditionally designated as the suq al-arba'a — the Wednesday market, and nine others are located on the out-skirts of the market area. With one or two exceptions, the person who sits in the stall, who accepts orders, sells the jewelry, does minor repairs and the like is himself the owner of the stall. He may be working with the capital invested by a parent, relative or associate but the major share of the proceeds will belong to him. No matter what ties may exist between the owners of these stalls, including those of kinship, each stall is an independent commercial unit, and each merchant is looking out for his own profit.

How does this system work? How can so many jewelers working in close proximity make an independent living? How does pricing work? How is it possible to avoid collusion?

One cannot understand the internal structure of this market simply in economic terms. Its forms and its integration make sense only when seen against a general social background, particularly those ethnic and commercial ties, such as the clientalization of exchange, which modify and expand the purely economic aspects of competition. It gives rise to a system combining competition and collaboration, one which allows everyone a chance. It does not guarantee economic success, but everyone has an opportunity with skill and sharpness to make his way.

All the shops in the market carry the same or similar items. Some specialize in certain types of ornaments, such as coral jewelry or ankle bracelets or necklaces. Some have a larger

114

Above: the jewelry market in Houmt Souk. *Below:* a jewelled headband and necklace: simultaneously an ornament, a prophylactic device and stored wealth.

selection than others, but the basic tiems — bracelets, necklaces, earrings and rings are found in most shops. Prices for these items in the various shops vary within a fairly narrow range. Two factors determine the price of any object: its weight, i.e. the amount and quality of gold and silver it contains; and the type of workmanship required to produce it. Workmanship is calculated by the gram, and its price varies according to the degree of sophistication. Simple

115

objects, such as gold chains, cost less per gram than more complex jewels with filigree and fine granulation. Quality of workmanship, as distinct from its type, is a minor element in determining the price of a piece of jewelry. This system of pricing is known and accepted by all parties — producer, buyer and seller.

Although prices may vary somewhat from shop to shop, and although the bargaining process may modify prices even further, the competition in the jewelers' market is not for prices but is, in the eyes of the Jerbans themselves, a competition for clients. This view of their own activity confirms something which has been observed in other North African bazaars, namely, that exchange takes place through a "system of clientalization." That is, in the suq, a seller is not confronting an undifferentiated mass of potential buyers but is dealing with known, even habitual exchange partners. The same, of course, is true from the point of view of the buyer.

How does one create this relationship? Ma'tuq gives the following formula for the attraction of new clients: 1. a pleasant and welcoming manner, easy conversation, jokes, 2. reasonable prices — neither too high nor too low; 3. interesting merchandise, well-made, well-finished and attractive looking; 4. honest and accurate quality, especially with respect to the quality of the precious metal and the weight; 5. reliability — if you don't have certain merchandise and you promise it to a client, you must indeed have it ready and available at the time promised; 6. generosity and flexibility in accepting goods back from clients. This is especially important since men frequently purchase the jewelry for their womenfolk, who are occasionally displeased with the purchase. One must therefore accept goods returned by clients cheerfully and graciously.

The relationship between the Jewish seller and the Muslim buyer involves a certain degree of trust and familiarity, and a whole series of mutually understood and accepted expectations. In fulfilling these conditions, the merchant and the client have not only struck a deal, but have concluded an alliance which binds the future of both parties. For the merchant, this tacit pact leads to the extension of credit, to the acceptance of deferred or installment payments and to the consignment of merchandise without any deposit or receipt. For his part, the client owes not only loyalty, but is also supposed to serve as a mediator between the jeweler and other members of his family and, more generally, his whole social network.

By its very nature, this system is not capable of indefinite extension. The number of clients with whom a jeweler can maintain this degree of trust and familiarity is necessarily limited and thus encourages a fragmented system of exchange. Given sufficient demand, this pattern provides a socio-economic explanation for the proliferation of shops. The jewelers themselves explain the system in terms of the internal need and equilibrium of the community. Proliferation of the number of shops offers more young jewelers the opportunity both for greater independence and a greater share of prosperity. But it is also the mode of interaction with the external world which organizes the traditional system of exchange. Financially powerful shop owners are not tempted to reduce their prices and increase their volume by attracting customers from their less powerful colleagues. The nature of the relationship between merchants and clients would make such a policy difficult if not impossible to implement. Neither buyer nor seller would find it comfortable or advantageous. Similar considerations are at work in maintaining the large number of independent artisan-jewelers working within the confines of the Hara. In the summer of 1979, there were over 45 independent artisans in the Hara producing objects for the shops in Houmt Souk from their workshops, which for the most part are located in their own homes. In addition there are approximately 20 young boys who are at various stages of apprenticeship assisting these craftsmen and who in the space of a few years will establish their own workshops. This proliferation of independent production (one finds several instances of two or more independent workshops in the same family household — father and son, or brothers working separately) is nurtured by the same economic and social factors which support the numerous retail jewelry establishments in Houmt Souk.

116

Here, the clientalization of exchange does not cross ethnic boundaries but takes place between the Jewish producers in the Hara and their coreligionist merchant-distributors in the suq. A large part of the surplus capital of the merchants in the suq is channeled to finance the jewelry production of the Hara. But here again, the form that this investment activity takes is profoundly influenced by the traditional social needs and practices of the community. The leading merchants in the suq have sought neither the linear integration of the jewelry business which would transform the independent artisans in the Hara dependent on their purchases into their employees, nor the rationalization of the production of jewels by setting up factories with modern, but expensive, labor and time-saving equipment. The investment is distributed among virtually all the craftsmen in the Hara, many of whom have developed specializations in the production of certain types of jewelry, or even of individual components of more complex jewelry. This investment is also consciously distributed throughout the year, with its flow more ample during the slow months following the Muslim festivals or following the traditional season for marriages. In redistributing work among the artisan-jewelers, the merchants are also contributing to the regulation of the market.

For richer merchants, there are advantages to this form of organization that would disappear with the linear integration of jewelry production and distribution. In the present system, they enjoy a double benefit. By investing their capital in many small operations they both decrease their risks and increase their ability to conceal a part of their activities. Their stalls in Houmt Souk are, commercially, only the tip of the iceberg. But the numerous business dealings which connect merchants to their clients and to other merchants and artisans escape easy detection or control. The ultimate symbol of this crypto-economy is the form of their accounts. Most accounts are kept orally; debts and credits are stored in each jeweler's memory. When they do resort to writing, the scraps of paper which they use as aide-memoires are written in a local script which only the Jewish jewelers are able to decipher.

Haqq al-Yahud
A Password between Jews and Arabs

There is no single generalization or rule which could serve to characterize the whole range of social and economic contacts between Jerban Jews and Jerban Muslims. Each circumstance of contact between them has its own movable boundaries in which elements of friendship and hostility, confidence and suspicion, collaboration and competition are intermingled in varying proportions. In the market, the notion which governs commerce between Jews and Muslims is that of *haqq al-yahud*, a concept which has many meanings and uses, but which translated literally means "the law, the justice, the honesty of Jews." It is not surprising to find this quality invoked by the Jews themselves. But it is also invoked by Muslims as a password to cut short any bargaining or other negotiations concerning the price or quality of an object. Concluding a discussion with the invocation of haqq al-yahud is equivalent to giving an oath. The Jewish jeweler places his honesty, his reputation, his reliability on the line — that is, all the qualities which form the basis of his relationship with his clients. But, this is more than a personal engagement; it is, at the same time, that of the group to which the jeweler belongs. Beyond the single moral quality of honesty — individual and collective — there is also the reference to respect for the law. Put in another way, since the *ahl al-kitab* are people of the law, one can deal with them.

Haqq al-yahud implies a long list of qualities: skill and reliability in performing work, honesty in transactions and in keeping accounts. This notion summarizes the good relations between buyers and sellers. Needless to say, this ideal of mercantile ethics does not necessarily reflect the reality of the Jerban market. It is primarily the Jews who attribute to the haqq al-yahud their success in the market place. But even Muslims accept this image, because it marks the limits which Jewish merchants cannot violate in their commercial practice.

117

Thus the notion of haqq al-yahud takes us beyond a simple ecological explanation of the Jewish role in Jerban economy, that it simply fulfills a social and cultural need or only provides goods and services for which there is a demand. Rather, it expresses a vision of organic integration into a system of life in which the fact of their Jewishness becomes a paramount element even in the mundane pursuit of their daily bread and the basis for their relations with Muslims.

For the notions of reliability and honesty implied by the phrase haqq al-yahud have their counterpart in the value system internal to the Jewish community itself. The anecdotes and miracle stories of their rabbis and holy men highlight most prominently and most consistently their reliability and faith (Hebrew: *imun*) and absolute uprightness and integrity (Hebrew: *yashar*). It is not only personal honesty which these stories emphasize, but rather the quality of uncompromising, consistent adherence to moral and religious principles. It is to this unwavering, single-minded religious integrity — exemplified by their rabbis — that the Jews of Jerba attribute their success in resisting assimilation and communal decay. For them it is this quality which enabled them to maintain a community which was and, in the view of many, still is the "Jerusalem of Africa". This dominant theme, rooted in their internal communal life, transformed and applied to their economic life and commercial contacts with Muslims, became the haqq al-yahud. Internally, these values contributed to the construction of a very specific Jerban "fence around the Torah"; externally, the values emanating from the inside serve to demarcate for them the movable boundaries of their everyday relations with non-Jews, and provide the bridge between their complex, overlapping internal network and individual members of their neighboring communities.

1. C. GEERTZ, "The Bazaar of Sefrou" in C. GEERTZ, H. GEERTZ and L. ROSEN, *Meaning and Order in Moroccan Society*, Cambridge, 1979.
2. Boaz HADDAD, *Jerba Yehudit*, Jerusalem, 1978, p. 22.
3. Shushan HACOHEN, *Sefer Mamlekhet Kohanim*, Jerusalem, n.d., p. 328.
4. Boaz HADDAD, *Op. cit.* p. 22.
5. Boaz HADDAD, *Op. cit.* p. 12.
6. Victor FLEURY, *La Tunisie. Agriculture, industrie, commerce*, Vol. 1, 1900.

7
Pilgrimage to Jerba

In the caravanserai of the Ghriba.

The Synagogues of Jerba

At their peak, in the early 1950's the Jewish communities of Jerba had a combined population of 4500 inhabitants. To serve their devotional and other needs they maintained a group of no less than twenty synagogues, gathering places for worship, for study, for gossip, and for communal exchange. Since women do not attend, this translated into one synagogue for every hundred believers. In the past thirty years, several synagogues have been closed or used for other purposes. Today, with a drastically reduced Jewish population, seventeen synagogues remain in active use in Hara Kebira, Hara Sghira and Houmt Souk. The synagogue of Houmt Souk bears the name of its founders, the Parientes, a family of Italian nationality which prospered in Jerba during the second half of the 19th and early 20th century. Most of the Jewish families which inhabited the Taourit quarter around the synagogue have long since emigrated or moved back to Hara Kebira, their place of origin. Nevertheless, this synagogue, embedded in a compact block of houses and commercial buildings, is still in use.

Hara Kebira harbors eleven other synagogues. With names such as Sla Rebbi Bezalel, Sla Rebbi Eliezer, Sla Rebbi Brahem, Trabelsiya, Dightiya, and so on, each recalls either the rabbi or the group of families who established it. In Dighet, where there are five, they are called *yeshivot*, places of study, since in that village the synagogue par excellence is of course the Ghriba.

Because of its isolated location, the successive expansions it has undergone, and its role as a site of pilgrimage and tourism, the Ghriba exhibits characteristics very different from those of other synagogues. All other Jerban synagogues follow a similar plan, as if a single

Interior of the synagogue of Rebbi Brahem in Hara Kebira.

architect had conceived their layout, their volume and their decoration. The exact same model is encountered in Ben Gardane, Zarzis, and the other communities which constitute what we have called the Jerban archipelago.

The most remarkable element of these synagogues is that they are double structures, with one room open to the sky attached to a second larger covered room. The rooms are parallel to one another and are both oriented toward Jerusalem. Jerbans say that this doubling has a seasonal explanation. The open space is appropriate to the summer, including the Festival of Tabernacles, when a part of the courtyard is covered with palm branches to celebrate Succoth. During the winter, the congregation retires inside to the second room. But in fact, both winter and summer, the two rooms make it possible to have two *minyans* — the ten men required to perform a service — and to conduct two services simultaneously. The *heikhal*, the cabinet which contains the Torah scrolls, is situated at the end of the covered room. Silver plaques in the shape of fish, censers, hands or tablets of the law are attached to the doors of the ark. These plaques are invariably dedicated to the memory of deceased individuals. Windows pierce the walls which, in the more richly decorated synagogues, are usually covered with blue tiles. Along the walls, stand benches covered with matting, on which the congregants rest, study or slumber, and above these are rows of hooks from which the lamps commemorating the dead are hung. With its *ex-votos* and its oil lamps, the synagogue has become the custodian of the memory of the dead, even more so than the cemetery which the Jews of Jerba seldom visit. Here a marble slab, there a simple sheet of framed paper give the names of deceased believers who have donated gifts to the synagogue. Collection-boxes, bolted shut, are attached to the wall, one to benefit the rabbis of the Holy Land, another for the society which supports the schools, a third for the organization which used to combat the annual invasion of scorpions. Lamps for Rebbi Shem'un and Rebbi Meir,

Synagogue of Rebbi Brahem in Hara Sghira.

121

sometimes together with those honoring the memory of great local rabbis, are present in every synagogue (figure 10).

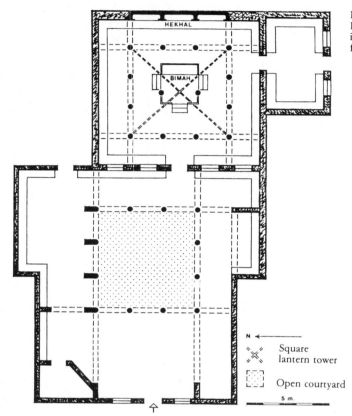

Figure 10:
Plan of the Hizkiyahu Synagogue
in Hara Kebira
following Pinkerfeld.

A majority of the synagogues in the two villages and in the neighboring communities are crowned by a kind of lantern tower in the shape of a cube whose sides are punctuated by colored-glass windows. These windows recall the twelve tribes of Israel, whose names are written inside the synagogue. Only one synagogue in Hara Kebira, the Sla al-Kabir (Great Synagogue) is without this lantern tower. Several small synagogues of Hara Sghira which also lack this superstructure might bear witness to a time when the Jews were denied the right to construct ostentatious places of worship. In the Trabelsiya synagogue of Hara Sghira, the narrow openings which barely allow a little bit of sky to show through can hardly be called windows. Its white-washed walls are bare and only its Torah cabinets, built from carved wood, show any traces of art or skill. Here austerity has reached an extreme point. Even in other synagogues, simplicity approaches severity. The light in them is blue, reflected from the glazed tiles which cover the walls, from the paint on the ceiling and the columns, and from the colored glass on the windows. Only these tiles, the woodwork, a few objects used in worship (the reading hand, and silver *ex-votos*) and, occasionally, the chandeliers, are meant to be decorative. A serious mood generally prevails.

The synagogue usually lies at the center of a complex of buildings which serve several communal purposes. Quite a number are adjacent to cemeteries, as is the case with the

The synagogue of Rebbi Eliezer in Hara Kebira: the ceiling of painted wood.

Ghriba, and the synagogues of Rebbi Shalom, Rebbi Brahem and the Great Synagogue of Hara Kebira. One in Dighet, and two in Hara Kebira were seats of the local rabbinic court which convened in a separate room or group of rooms attached to the synagogues. Their walls, which are still lined with books and codes of law, preserve the vestiges of former deliberations. More often, synagogues are surrounded by study rooms and libraries for the use of students or pious men.

The Ghriba

The Ghriba is the only synagogue with a reputation beyond Jerba. It receives large numbers of pilgrims for *Lag Ba'omer* and visits from local Jews throughout the year. For tourists, stopping at the Ghriba is part of the required program for seeing the island.

When Nahum Slouschz described it at the beginning of this century, it had recently undergone some transformations. "I am told," he said, "that the building was rebuilt around 40 years ago, and that all the tombstones which could be found in the cemetery next to the walls of the holy house were used in its construction". In the 60's or 70's of the 19th century, the Ghriba had already been enlarged. In those days, it looked like "a square building, rather sober in appearance, and completely lacking in style ... Inside, dark hallways are followed by a square nave, in the middle of which is an 'Almenor' and on top of which is a gallery, held up by columns: nothing specific, nothing characteristic".[1] Since Slouschz made his visit, a room, serving as an antechamber, has been added. It is oblong, and

123

from it one enters the sanctuary itself. The Ghriba lacks the open-air prayer room which the other synagogues have. Similarly, because of many structural modifications, its upper windows are more numerous than the tribes of Israel, and have lost all their symbolic meaning.

The Ghriba is also a hostel or inn. At the end of the last century, a large and spacious *oukala* was erected to receive pilgrims. In the 1950's, at a time when it seemed that the pilgrimage would continue to expand, the Jerbans built a second caravanserai, principally intended to accommodate Libyan pilgrims. However, the Libyan communities had begun to disintegrate after 1948 and, following anti-Jewish incidents after the six-day war, the last Jews left Libya in 1967. Therefore, the second caravanserai was never actually used. Some former residents of Tripoli do make the pilgrimage to Jerba from Rome, where they now live. Their numbers are small, and changed habits and the development of tourism on the island tend to bring them to the beachfront hotels rather than to the oukala.

Since the architectural aspects of the Ghriba have been studied at length and with great learning there is no need for a prolonged description.[2] Nor will we dwell on the fact that, as has often been observed, there are several other sanctuaries throughout the Maghreb which resemble this lonely Ghriba and which are called by the same name. Slouschz counted six of them in Libya, Tunisia and Algeria, and his inventory was incomplete.

There are apparently contradictory legends concerning the synagogue's name and its site. The first of these relates that the island seemed strange and marvelous (Arabic: *ghriba*) to the Jews who, after their flight from Palestine, came here to found a synagogue.

This version of the synagogue's beginnings accords with the myth of origin of the community of Hara Sghira. Its principal actors are the kohanim, the refugee priests from Jerusalem who carried with them a piece of the destroyed Temple. The second legend accounts only for the beginnings of the synagogue and not for those of the community. Its heroine is a young girl who was alone in a foreign land (once again Arabic: *ghriba*). According to Slouschz,[3] who reported what the learned men of Jerba told him at the beginning of this century, the place where the Ghriba now stands was once a deserted, isolated hill, ignored by the inhabitants of Hara Sghira. One day, to their great surprise, they found that a beautiful young girl had settled there. She was modest and virtuous and lived alone in a hut of branches. She had about her an aura of purity and holiness and, out of deference to her, no one approached to find out where she came from, why she was there, or how she lived. One evening, the people of Hara Sghira saw flames shooting up from her hut. They were afraid that she might be performing some kind of magic and no one dared approach the fire. After it subsided, some of them went to the place. They found that the hut had been reduced to ashes, and that the girl had died. Yet her body was untouched and the fire had not changed her features. They then understood that she had been a saint, that they should have helped her in her solitude, and that they should have acknowledged her holy character. They built a synagogue at the site of the hut to commemorate the marvelous foreign girl.

Passed on by word of mouth, the legend has changed with time. "No one ever heard her voice ... they were afraid of her, they ran away from her," wrote Emmanuel Grevin in 1937.[4] Forty years later, a woman on the pilgrimage told another story which resolves the contradiction between the two versions already reported. The ghriba was a young Jewish girl who managed to escape from Palestine alone on a fragile raft, holding the scrolls of the Torah to her heart. Driven by the winds, she reached the shores of Jerba, and fell down exhausted at the place where the synagogue was later built.

In this last version, at least, the girl is Jewish. In the story reported by Slouschz, and taken up by other Jerban authors, there is nothing to identify this mysterious girl, who has neither name nor family.

In any case, the residents of Dighet built the synagogue in her honor. Indeed, the Ghriba is their only complete synagogue, since it alone, to the exclusion of all others in Dighet, can house the scrolls of the Torah. It is maintained by an administrative committee which was founded at the beginning of the French Protectorate and which is completely independent of the religious authorities of the two villages. The members of the Ghriba committee are recruited from among the inhabitants of Hara Sghira. It is they who collect and manage the proceeds generated by the pilgrimage, by contributions made during the rest of the year, and from the rent of lands and shops owned by the Ghriba. Every Thursday afternoon, they distribute part of these revenues as a stipend to the permanent readers who spend their days reciting Psalms and reading the Zohar in the synagogue. In addition to their stipend, these *batlanim* receive a supplement in proportion to the size of their families and a portion of the small gifts left by visitors at the synagogue. Up until the fifties, there were always several dozen permanent readers chosen from among the men of Dighet on the basis of their knowledge, their moral qualities and their economic need. In those days, their prayers filled the synagogue. Now they have been reduced to a college of ten members recruited mainly for their inability to perform any other function.

The inhabitants of Hara Kebira view the appropriation of the Ghriba by the people of Hara Sghira with considerable ambiguity and misgiving. On the one hand, they share in the sanctuary's veneration. To ward off misfortune, the families of Hara Kebira have recourse to the Ghriba, offering a meal to its readers. As we shall soon see, the Ghriba figures in their marriage ritual. One of Hara Kebira's revered rabbis of the recent past, Rabbi Moshe Aydan, would regularly conclude his fasts and acts of penance by walking the seven kilometers from Hara Kebira to the Ghriba in order to spend several hours there in study and prayer. On the other hand, the pilgrimage which has grown around the Ghriba has conferred considerable prestige upon Hara Sghira, the legitimacy of which is seriously questioned in Hara Kebira. The pilgrimage has also generated considerable revenues to which the residents of Hara Kebira have no access. Thus, the Ghriba is one of the stakes in the ongoing rivalry between the two villages. Even though they partake fully and openly in the pilgrimage festivities and ceremonies, the inhabitants of Hara Kebira object to what they consider profane excesses, such as the mixing of men and women, the doubtful purity of the food eaten by the pilgrims in the hotels, and the noisy, questionable goings-on for which the pilgrimage provides an occasion.

The Procession of the Ghriba

It is not known when the Ghriba was first venerated outside of Jerba. Testimonials to the prestige of this synagogue begin to appear only in the second half of the 19th century. Even the Muslims recognized its holy character. Slowly, it began to attract the pious from Libya and Tunisia in ever larger numbers. Possibly, it was the Jerban Jewish emigrés who were responsible for spreading this cult when they settled in these regions.

The pilgrimage to the Ghriba takes place one month after Passover and culminates on Lag Ba'omer, 33 days after Passover. It continues between the 14th of *Iyyar*, commemorating the death of Rebbi Meir, and the 18th, which celebrates the *hillula* of Rebbi Shem'un. It attracts merchants, beggars and pilgrims. Merchants bid at an auction for the right to have their shops in the caravansarai and hasten to set up stands for roast meat, drinks and fried *briks*. Itinerant merchants, Jewish or Muslim, make space for themselves in the courtyard, to display fruit, clothing, books or souvenirs. Beggars come from as far away as Tunis, sure that they will more than recover their travel expenses. As for the pilgrims, they come in a constant stream. At first they devote themselves to solitary worship. Every pilgrim comes to the Ghriba, enters its outer hall, takes off his shoes and covers his head, and then continues to the inner sanctuary. There, everyone lights a candle and makes a silent vow, and offers a small contribution to a member of the Ghriba committee, who is permanently installed in the synagogue for the duration of the pilgrimage and who writes out a receipt for every donation collected. Pilgrims also deposit envelopes containing contributions entrusted to

125

them by their friends and relatives, and they take a receipt made out to the donor. Everyone keeps an exact account of receipts and expenditures.

The pilgrims continue to make their way through the synagogue, whether merely to kiss the Torah ark, or to make a second set of vows. Under the ark there is an alcove illuminated by candles. Tradition designates it as the spot where the mysterious girl's body was found. People place a raw egg, and sometimes several raw eggs, in this small cave. On each is written the name of an unmarried but eligible girl. At the end of the several days of ceremonies, each pilgrim retrieves his or her egg which has now been baked by the candles' heat. It is brought back to the girl in question who, after consuming it, is assured of finding a husband within the year.

After circumambulating the sanctuary, the pilgrims are led back to the outer hall. Here they celebrate a *sh'uda*. They pay one of the readers of the Ghriba to recite a prayer, after which they distribute dried fruit and glasses of spirits to the assembled company. Whatever remains at the bottom of the glass is poured back into the bottle. This bottle is hastily resealed and, together with the dried fruit, is taken back to the pilgrim's home and its blessing shared with the members of the family who did not make the trip.

During the first days of the pilgrimage, the native Jerbans greet, accompany, follow and serve the pilgrims. Since they have access to the Ghriba at every moment of their lives, they do not have to wait for the pilgrimage to call upon her intercession. Indigenous participation in the pilgrimage becomes full and active only on the 17th and 18th of Iyyar, when the *menara*, the large candelabrum, is taken out of its storage place, sumptuously decorated and borne in procession to Hara Sghira. At that time a large crowd fills the courtyard and the

Annual pilgrimage to the Ghriba. The chariot of the *menara* being readied like a bride for the procession.

galleries of the caravanserai. Women and girls covered by jewelry come out and take their places in the upper galleries. Only on this occasion do the Jews of Hara Kebira condescend to come to Dighet accompanied by their wives and children. The Jews of Zarzis and tatahouine also come to take part in the procession, as do Muslim men and women who join the crowd as spectators.

The menara is a hexagonal pyramid, skillfully mounted on three wheels. It spends the entire year stored in a room at the caravanserai. Its five levels represent the Jerban view of the hierarchy of beings. At the base are the Jewish people made up of the twelve tribes of Israel; then come the various famous rabbis of Tunisia whose names mingle at the third level with those of important biblical personages, such as Abraham, Isaac, Rachel and Leah. At the top of the third level an inscription in Hebrew letters reads: "This candelabrum is in honor of Rebbi Meir Ba'al Hanes and Rebbi Shem'un Bar Yohai, may their merits assure us of protection." Over this, the name of God, *Shaddai*, is inscribed in a star of David, and then, finally, the tablets of the Law, in silver, crown the whole construction.

Before the procession, the menara is wrapped, covered and hidden under several layers of silk and muslin kerchiefs. These fabrics, as well as the *rimonim* (silver globes in the form of pomegranates) which are attached to the top of the menara are the objects of a very lively and raucous auction that takes place in the courtyard of the caravanserai, accompanied by music from the local orchestra and ululations from the women's gallery. At every transaction, the women generously sprinkle both the menara and the assembled pilgrims standing around it with scented water, while the auctioneers down glasses filled to the brim with spirits. After the last piece of silk has been sold, a slow procession sets out, accompanying

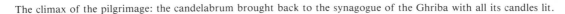

The climax of the pilgrimage: the candelabrum brought back to the synagogue of the Ghriba with all its candles lit.

127

the menara on its journey of one kilometer from the caravanserai to Dighet. The privilege of carrying it for a few yards is again offered to the highest bidder. The procession therefore is interrupted by countless stops, and takes hours to cover the short distance between the synagogue and the village. With the orchestra forming the vanguard, pilgrims surround and follow the menara while young Muslims join the procession, and a few cars bring up the rear of the parade.

Once it reaches the village, the procession with the menara stops briefly at each synagogue for a prayer service, and then returns to the Ghriba, arriving there as darkness falls. The menara is brought into the synagogue and all its candles are lit. People eat fruit, fresh almonds, sunflower seeds and liberally imbibe drinks. This is one of the rare occasions when there is no separation of men from women, of children from adults, of Jews of the great Hara from those of the little Hara, of Muslims from Jews, nor of natives from foreigners. The barriers, so rigorously maintained by Jerban Jews, are lowered for this celebration. On the following day, the 18th of Iyyar, the procession is repeated. The menara is then once again relegated to its storage place in the caravanserai for another year, and the pilgrims return home.

The Ghriba in Exile

What do these pilgrims expect, and what do they take back with them from this voluntary journey which is not required by religion? Why come from so far away to a place which is not the Promised Land? At first glance, the pilgrimage is a form of tourism, a simple commercial operation which is lucrative for the travel agencies that organize it. It can be seen as an excuse for the people who make the trip to have themselves some fun. And it is true that the trip to Jerba has, depending on the pilgrims' age, the character of "a week's paid vacation," or "a senior citizens' excursion." Indeed, spiritual activity is nearly nonexistent. There are neither prayers, nor meditations on the pilgrims' part. In fact, everything is bought, from the airplane ticket and the hotel room to the rabbis' blessings, the prayers for the dead, the intercession of the Ghriba and the mitzvot of the menara.

Like other trips of this kind, a visit to Jerba offers the illusion of social inversion, of a suspension of the normal order of things. Rest, games and a holiday atmosphere win out over work. The pleasures of night life win out over daytime tasks, and ostentatious spending, indeed waste, takes the place of the hard-working calculations of daily life. As at a carnival, one feels rich during this holiday, one is like a king, *kini beyyet*, like the Bey himself. On this pilgrimage, the women greatly outnumber the men. Away from their homes, their husbands and children, they give themselves over to dance, to song, to showing off their clothing. "We are like lionesses let loose from their chains," said one of them, with evident satisfaction.

Is this a vacation after all, a kind of carnival? No, it is more than that. Jerba in May is something else. Let us go through the itinerary once again. We should read this journey somewhat differently.

The date of the pilgrimage corresponds to Lag Ba'omer, celebrated among most Jews because an epidemic among the disciples of Akiba, the famous rabbi of the second century, is supposed to have abated on that day. In addition. Rebbi Meir is supposed to have died on the 14th of Iyyar, and Rebbi Shem'un on the 18th. Both were disciples of Akiba. Confusing the two elements, the Jews of Tunisia attribute the end of a terrible indigenous epidemic to the two rabbis.

On another level, the authorship of the Zohar, "The Book of Splendor," the very basis of kabbalistic mysticism, is attributed to Rebbi Shem'un. Scholars have established that the book was, in fact, the work of a Spaniard in the thirteenth century, but for the Jews of North Africa, as for orthodox Jews elsewhere, it was revealed to Rebbi Shem'un who transmitted it to some of his disciples.

A fervent cult has grown around these two second-century rabbis throughout the Maghreb and in Palestine. So deeply is it anchored in North African memory that people believe that the rabbis themselves were Maghrebis. In 1955, one could read in the major daily newspaper of Tunis, *La Presse*, that Rebbi Meir and Rebbi Shem'un "exercised their priestly functions in the synagogue of 'the Ghriba,' and died there in a state of holiness." They had been miracle workers, they remained miracle workers, and once they were dead they could still receive appeals for help from Jews in distress. Success in an examination for the certificate of primary studies, a child's recovery from a disease, the return of a son who had gone off to fight during the Second World War, all were due to Rebbi Shem'un's inter- cession. This debt was acknowledged every year by a private celebration and a public offering. Within the home, the families mark this occasion with a festive meal for their relatives, friends and neighbors, accompanied by the strains of the hymn Bar Yohai. Houses are decorated with garlands and illuminated by lamps and candles. The public cult was combined with the veneration of other purely local rabbis such as Rebbi Amran ben Diwan in Wazzan, Rebbi Ephraim Enkaoua in Tlemcen, or, finally, the Ghriba of Jerba. The hillula of Rebbi Shem'un involved a pilgrimage to these saints' tombs, and a night spent reciting prayers and Psalms and reading the Zohar near large, lit braziers next to the tomb.

This visit to Jewish saints' tombs evokes another practice which is very widespread in the Maghreb: the annual *ziyara* performed by the Muslims at the tombs of marabouts. In both cases, women play a very important part, since the mosque, like the synagogue, is primarily the domain of the men. In both cases, the distribution of food, the praying, the singing and the lighting of fires unite the pilgrims in a collective ceremony.

To make the journey to Jerba is, therefore, to continue a tradition, to repeat today what one's grandparents used to do, to nourish the same hopes, to expect the same benefits and to give thanks for them through the same rituals. This tradition's regional nature was already very strong before the emigration of the North African Jews. Each community or group of communities had its own particular rallying point. More recently, this regionalism has grown even stronger. The cult of saints, which one shares only with one's own, is becoming more and more local. The Tlemcen Jews return to Tlemcen, the ones from Constantine now make the celebration of the death of Rebbi Fradji coincide with the hillula of Rebbi Shem'un, so that they travel to Algeria, while the Tunisian Jews go to the Ghriba. In doing this, the pilgrims once again maintain a tradition, that of adhering to a locally-based cult without which the Eternal Omnipotent One would seem abstract, impersonal, and beyond reach. The pilgrimage, therefore, does not belong to world Judaism, but rather to the most narrowly regional Judaism.

But isn't there a paradox, a certain lack of balance, in converging from places like Rome, Montreal or Paris, to keep such a tradition alive? The long distances and the large crowds call for a third reading of the pilgrimage, one which does not negate the first two, but which completes them.

Let us imagine Tunis, Sousse or Sfax in the 1940's or 1950's with their Jewish com- munities still intact. These communities had their own space. Though certainly not confined to ghettos, the Jews tended to concentrate in certain areas while the Muslim Tunisians, the French, the Maltese and the Italians did the same in other distinct neighborhoods. There were businesses run by Jews, kosher butchers, synagogues, houses full of relatives, friends and memories. Everything nourished the feeling of homogeneity, of security, of continuity and of familiarity. At home, there were mezuzot attached to the doors. At the synagogue, families kept oil lamps for their dead. On the first Friday of the lunar month, the women would go to the cemetery. As in Jerba today, space was marked out with Jewish symbols, and time was measured to the rhythm of religious prescriptions. Out of all this, only frag- ments were retained once North Africa was left behind. Only remnants of this ambiance could be preserved or reconstituted in such Parisian neighborhoods as Belleville or Sarcelles. The statement repeated so often, that in the streets of those districts "you would think you were in Tunis" reveals that in fact you are not there any longer, that something or someone is missing from the picture.

Wherever the Maghrebi Jews have settled, the rhythm of secular time, that of work and economic activity, has triumphed over religious time. Each family or individual chooses some pieces to preserve and perpetuate. Someone fasts on Yom Kippur, someone else observes Passover.

Under these conditions, the recreation of the Jerba pilgrimage becomes a *re*-creation. For the duration of a week, a religious element is brought back into lives which have been deprived of it. People participate in a sort of general assembly during which they regroup the scattered community. At that time, Jerba assumes a particular quality which was previously denied it. It is perceived as the place where the Jews have been able to maintain their identity and their cohesion as a community without either of these entering into conflict with the realities of daily life. People no longer say that the Jerbans are "backward," but, more positively, that they are "very religious". They nourish the nostalgia for a place and a time free of today's contradictions — indeed, there were others, but who wants to remember?

The airplane which take pilgrims to Jerba is a machine for going back in time, and Jerba is the place of reunion. What you find there is yourself, and the *membra disjecta* of the lost community. Not only does the Ghriba get the girls married, she also eases the pain of *wahsh wal-ghorba*, the homesickness and pain of exile.

From this point of view, the pilgrimage is part of a broader phenomenon of religious and ethnic revival among Jews from North Africa. From Israel to Morocco, other commemorative rituals bring together Jews of the same origin, gathering them around old or new pilgrimage sites. All of them express the same aspirations and the same nostalgias. These religious ceremonies are expressions of a social aspiration: the aspiration of belonging to an integrated group, and not simply to exist as an atom in a society in which one participates without really belonging. In Israel, they have also become, as S. Deshen and M. Shokeid have shrewdly observed, a political discourse, a self-rehabilitation, in the context not only of uprootedness, but also of *déclassement* and of cultural domination. It is an attempt to reconcile a tradition, which is becoming less and less possible to practice, with the host culture.[5]

The Hillula, a Wedding Feast

To the various levels of meaning we have attributed to the pilgrimage, we must add yet another layer, one which applies only to the indigenous Jewish inhabitants of the island. In order to discern this meaning we must look at the two villages once again and follow the menara procession for the last time.

In each of the communities, as we have seen, man and woman constitute an asymmetric pair. Women are invested with fewer signs of Jewish identity than are the men of Jerba. From the moment of their circumcision, Jewish men bear the mark of their membership on their bodies, while the girls have no visible trace of their religious adherence. The girls are given secular first names more often than the boys. The clothing they wear before they get married is not different from that worn by the Muslim girls. Until the establishment some 30 years ago of the community school, women had no access to sacred texts, and the only language at their disposal was the vernacular. And finally, the synagogue is off limits to them. Yet, even though they are not the bearers of religion, they are the final refuge of the holy. Until recently, they were kept confined to the Hara and were protected from all contact with non-Jews. They occupied the forbidden, inviolable and sacred space of the Hara and the home.

The two villages, in their turn, form a pair whose elements complement one another and manifest the same ambivalence. Hara Sghira, which provides women to the other community and which is inhabited by kohanim, occupies the femine, sacred pole. From this point of view, the Ghriba represents the holy of holies. Not only the two villages, but even the Muslims accept its sacred character. Sacred, because a fragment of the Temple has been incorporated into its foundations. Sacred, also, because of the presence of the mysterious young girl. And the very place where the fragment of the Temple is to be found is a navel, whose heat is enough to cook the eggs left by the pilgrims in order to make their daughters marriageable. This ambivalent nature of the Ghriba also appears in the celebrations which take place in the synagogue. The men of Hara Sghira must go there three times a week, and during the major festivals, because the Ghriba is their only synagogue in the full sense of the term. But it is also the only one which the women frequent regularly. Each Thursday, they gather in large numbers to clean it and prepare it for the Sabbath. Following this chore, they walk in procession through the synagogue, lighting oil lamps and spreading incense until they reach the three main lamps hung before the Torah cabinet. One of these is dedicated to Rebbi Meir, the second to Rebbi Shem'un, and the third is called the *Sibiya*, the young girl. This is the only case in which the two masters of the mystical tradition are accompanied by a young virgin girl, solitary and unknown, who gave her name to the Ghriba. Once the lamp of the Sibyia has been lit, the women rest under this lamp, lying on the ground before going their separate ways to prepare for the Sabbath. Young newlyweds from Dighet and Hara Kebira present themselves before this very same lamp on the day after the consummation of their marriage. They are accompanied by a cortege of relatives and friends, and with this visit the entire set of wedding ceremonies comes to an end.

What is the meaning of Lag Ba'omer in a context such as this? When the menara has been adorned, perfumed, decked with fabrics which veil it from people's sight, it resembles a young girl about to be brought to her bridegroom. In fact, it is called the *'arusa*, the bride. The itinerary that it follows from the Ghriba to the various yeshivot of Dighet, which are so many masculine spaces, is comparable to the procession leading the bride from her father's to her husband's house. The procession of the Ghriba celebrates a wedding, the symbolic union of the masculine and feminine principles within Hara Sghira, and the marriage between Hara Sghira and Hara Kebira.

But there is more. The occasion of this celebration is the death of Rebbi Shem'un which is designated as a hillula, a wedding, since the master of the Zohar went to meet his God on that day. One of the major themes of Zoharic mysticism is that of the mystical marriage of the community with its Lord, through which the hidden meaning of the Divine Word becomes revealed in its infinite fullness. In Zoharic symbolism, the community represents the feminine principle, and God the masculine principle. In Jerba, to lead the menara clad in a bride's finery in a procession is, in the end, to lead the community to meet its Lord.

1. N. SLOUSCHZ, *Un voyage d'études juives en Afrique*, Paris, 1909.
2. J. PINKERFELD, "Un témoignage du passé en voie de disparition: les synagogues de la région de Djerba," *Cahiers de Byrsa*, 1957, VII, pp. 127–188.
3. N. SLOUCHZ, *Ha-i Peli*, Tel Aviv, 1957.
4. E. GREVIN, *Djerba, l'île heureuse, et le Sud tunisien*, Paris, 1937.
5. S. DESHEN and M. SHOKEID, *The Predicament of Homecoming Cultural and Social Life of North African Immigrants in Israel*, Ithaca, 1974.

8
Epilogue

Letter from Jerba, March 27, 1981:

> It was a minor incident that took place this very evening with a non-Jew, petty, but of deep significance. I ordered a metal plate from him to be affixed to my motorbike on which my name and address were to be painted. He, however, changed the place name. Instead of Hara Kebira he wrote As-Sawani (Gardens). When I asked him why he made the change, he responded that it was its proper name. The name Hara Kebira is to be erased and not to be remembered or mentioned anymore. The municipal council and its president convened a special meeting on this question and decided to uproot the name of Hara Kebira and change it to As-Sawani. I argued with the man and insisted that for me its name was still Hara Kebira. Tomorrow, I intend to have the sign changed to read Hara Kebira.
>
> His response pained me deeply. I thought to myself: We Jews, who reached this place long before them, who have a history of more than two thousand years here, not only are they seeking to push us out, but they are even conspiring to erase our past and the names of famous Jewish places from history.

On the surface, the incident described in this letter is indeed a petty one. For some years now the non-Jewish population of Hara Kebira has been growing so that by now it accounts for more than half the residents. Thus, it is perhaps understandable that these newcomers and the administration, partially for reasons of their own and not necessarily because of any hostility to the older Jewish inhabitants, wished to change the name of this town to reflect its present demographic and cultural character. Whatever its motivation, this apparently innocent change in toponyms is perceived by the Jewish community as a political issue and a potential threat.

As we have pointed out throughout this book, the Jewish communities of Jerba have maintained practices and developed strategies to defend and adjust those of their traditions which have permitted them to endure. This policy was possible only in the historical circumstances of coexistence and exchange with the rest of the population, an interaction which allowed for constant readjustments and adequate responses to change. Are these conditions still in place? At present, local, national and international forces have pushed the Jews into a contradiction from which it is difficult to see how they can extricate themselves. On the local level, the nature of the society which surrounds them has been profoundly changed. The mosaic of ethnic, religious and agnatic groups which once existed is in the process of transformation into a nation striving for homogeneity. Within this new setting the Jews have become a minority.

This has given rise to a situation which is both critical and ambiguous. Critical because, like other groups in the rest of the world, a minority always ends up as a candidate for nationality.[1] Given that the state is neither pluralist nor secular, and given that the Jerban Jewish communities are not prepared to accept a process of secularization which would condemn them to extinction, any integration into the dominant society and culture is unthinkable. Jewish participation in the current political life of the country thus remains impossible.

The situation is rendered even more critical by developments external to the island to which Jews and Muslims react in an opposite manner. Echoes of events in the Middle East are distinctly audible in Jerba and complicate the relationship between the two groups.

The same young man writes in another letter:

> They say that the Jews are secure and have no problems whatsoever with their Muslim neighbors. But they forget all the stones that are thrown at Jewish individuals, at synagogues and Jewish homes, the spitting on Jewish places of worship and the shouts of insults and mockeries directed against Jews.

The acts enumerated in this letter have become common occurrences. In the face of these incidents the Jews feel powerless and do not even bother to register complaints with the police or other governmental authorities responsible for public order. After all, these officials belong to "the other group;" how then can they be expected to act fairly? Instead, they fall back upon the notion of exile, of *galut*, to which such humiliations are a natural accompaniment. To younger members of the community, the notion of galut now seems untenable and anachronistic. Our correspondent continues:

> The people of Israel is not a widower. The sun of the redemption has already risen. We will leave this place carrying with us our culture and our past.

If they leave the island, the Jerban Jews would also have to abandon their language, their costume, their elaborate system of local customs, their educational system and, contrary to what the author of this letter believes, their history, too, would be left behind. They would certainly keep their Judaism intact but they would forfeit their community. Even if they created a new one, it would inevitably be quite different.

Coming to terms with the galut, with their exile, means for the Jews of Jerba assuming the status of a minority by progressively diminishing their cultural distinctiveness. It means renouncing any claim to their own space or to the name which it bears, in the same way as they spontaneously modified their costume and their domestic architecture. It also means that by giving up, sooner or later, their system of education and the intellectual framework which it provided, they will have to confine religious practice to the family framework. As with many other Jewish groups, their Judaism would become a private affair maintaining only two inviolable barriers: the sexual taboos and the dietary restrictions. However, it is not at all clear whether such a retrenchment is possible without the support of a community. Whereas for other Tunisians nationality is not in conflict with communal solidarities or with adherence to Islam, Jerban Jews cannot be Tunisians and stay on in Tunisia except by preserving their communal existence.

The ambiguity of their present condition can be succinctly formulated. While in the broad Tunisian context they constitute a minority, within the perimeters of the island the Jews of Jerba remain a community. And it is precisely when the community is directly threatened that they revert to their most traditional mode by activating the tried and true paradigms of their past. We turn once more to the text of our young Jerban correspondent describing the inauguration of a synagogue which was burned and severely damaged in 1979. The fire was probably the result of a criminal, arsonist act and the Jews, comparing the event to the destruction of the Temple, had marked it with fasting and mourning. Eighteen months later, on a date corresponding to the festival of Hanukka, the Temple was reconsecrated in Jerba, which became once again the "antechamber of Jerusalem."

Life in the community here proceeds as usual. About two months ago, we celebrated the rededication of the synagogue R. Bezalel Hanimni of blessed memory. The doors of the *heikhal* (ark) were repaired, plastered and beautifully painted. Only the wooden ceiling in front of the heikhal, which was damaged by the fire, was left unrepaired as "a reminder of the destruction". Four scrolls of the Torah, bought from Jews of Sfax who had emigrated and which were left behind there, were placed in the heikhal. It is a pity that you were not among us for the celebration.

It was a wondrous celebration and a most impressive gathering of the people. It began at four o'clock in the afternoon and continued until ten o'clock in the evening. First, a Torah was taken from the house of Meqiqes. He was one of the people who paid for the Torahs. The procession then continued to the homes of the other individuals who had contributed to the purchase of the Torahs. And in each house there was wine and beans and beer for all who cared to enter and songs and praises to God, accompanied by drums and dances led by Y.B.

The entire population of the town — men, women and children — and also from Ben Gradane, Zarzis and Medenine participated in this festive occasion — a great assembly. We marched to all the synagogues of the town with songs and hymns — including national songs. And the non-Jews were looking on in silence. At last, we reached the synagogue of R. Bezalel where Rebbi M. pronounced a homily in honor of the event in which he mentioned the dedicated efforts of the officers of the synagogue and of other individuals who worked hard for the repair and improvement of the synagogue and for the replacement of the new torahs in the heikhal.

We still recall that terrible night in which the Torah was burned and the ark was laid waste, with the fire consuming all parts of the building as well as the parchment of the Torahs, and we were helpless, unable to save them. We still remember the magnitude of the disaster which occurred. We all stood dumb-struck, confused and trembling in the destroyed synagogue. Thanks be to God that the Blessed Name bestowed His grace upon us so that the synagogue and the arks were repaired, and the people contributed scrolls of the Torah. And on this night all of us, from the youngest to the oldest, stood rejoicing. It was a joy and gladness for the Jews. This was but a small restitution for that which happened — may it never happen again, amen.

See this wonder. In the morning and in the afternoon prior to the time fixed for the ceremony, the day was overcast and rainy with a cold wind blowing. But afterwards, the clouds dispersed and the sun shone forth. "This came from the Lord, it was wondrous in our eyes".

1. C. GEERTZ, "The Integrative Revolution", in *Old Societies and New States*, New York, 1963.

9
Images of Jerba

The Torah, in its case
of painted wood.

A Rabbi and printer
of Hara Kebira.

Shem'un, artisan-jeweller
of Hara Kebira.

145

Rebbi Fraji, an active member
of the community of Hara Kebira.
He supervises the school luncheons,
runs the communal grocery store,
and takes part, together with his jeweller son,
in one of the evening study seminars.

Detail from a fabric embroidered with threads of gold—
worn by the bride at the marriage.

"And these words which I command you this day shall be upon your heart
and you shall teach them diligently to your children,
and shall talk of them when you sit in your house,
and when you walk by the way,
and when you lie down and when you rise.
And you shall bind then as a sign upon your hand,
and they shall be as frontlets between your eyes."
(*Deuteronomy*, VI:6-8)

The *koufia*, head-dress covered with gold coins
with a "hand" attached to it.

A Jerban woman lights a candle and makes a vow during the pilgrimage of Sidi Youssef el-Ma'rabi.

A boy reading a book in the library
of his "family" synagogue.

Solitary study in the Ghriba.

A Jewish dyer in Houmt Souk:
the last representative of a once flourishing profession.

Hara Kebira: a craftsman in a workshop
set up in his own house.
Most of the tools of his trade
are visible in the immediate vicinity of this jeweller.
The bouquet of flowers
was not placed there by the photographer.

"Pomegranates" of silver
which crown the Torah.

165

Transporting the *menara*,
wrapped in silken fabrics,
from the Ghriba to Hara Sghira.

Offerings at the Ghriba.

One of the stops of the procession.
Gathering together the living and remembering the dead
in one of the synagogues of Hara Sghira.

Sources and Bibliography

The fieldwork on which this study is based was accomplished during three stays on the island of Jerba during the spring and summer of 1978 and 1979. In the summer of 1979, the authors were joined by a Tunisian photographer, Jacques Pérez, who did extensive photographic work in the two communities of the island for part of that summer and during the fall and winter of that year.

The information collected during our fieldwork is supplemented by data derived from the Civil Archives of Houmt Souk, the General Archives of the Government of Tunisia in Tunis, the archives of the Alliance Israélite in Paris and, most importantly, by the books published in the two Jerban communities.

Most Arabic and Hebrew terms used in the text follow their pronunciation in Jerba rather than their written classical form. E.g., *'inara* (the evil eye) instead of the literary *'ayn hara'*. For technical reasons, diacritical points and markers indicating long vowels have been omitted.

All the names used in this text are fictitious.

The following bibliography is selective:

N

ATTAL, Robert, *Les Juifs d'Afrique du Nord, bibliographie*, Jerusalem, 1973.

BENJAMIN II, J.J., *Eight Years in Asia and Africa from 1846 to 1855*, Hanover, 1859.

BOURDIEU, Pierre, "Le sens pratique," *Actes de la Recherche en Sciences Sociales*, February 1976, pp. 43–86.

CAZÈS, David, *Notes bibliographiques sur la littérature juive tunisienne*, Tunis, 1893.

CHOURAQUI, André, *Between East and West: A History of the Jews of North Africa*, Philadelphia, 1968.

DESHEN, Shlomo, "The Work of Tunisian Scholars in Israel," *American Ethnologist*, II, 1975, pp. 251–259.

DESHEN, Shlomo and SHOKEID, M., *The Predcament of Homecoming, Cultural and Social Life of North African Immigrants in Israel*, Ithaca, 1974.

FLEURY, Victor, *La Tunisie, Agriculture, Industrie, Commerce*, Vol. 1, Paris, 1900.

FRAENKEL, Jacqueline, *L'imprimerie hébraique à Djerba (Ètude bibliographique)*, Thèse polycopiéé, Paris, 2 vols., 1982.

GEERTZ, Clifford, "The Integrative Revolution" in *Old Societies and New States*, New York, 1963.

GEERTZ, Clifford, GEERTZ, Hildred and ROSEN, Lawrence, *Meaning and Order in Moroccan Society*, Cambridge, 1979.

GENDRE, F., "L'île de Djerba," *Revue tunisienne*, 1907, vol. 14, pp. 504–522; 1908, vol. 15, pp. 60–79.

GOITEIN, S. D., *A Mediterranean Society, the Jewish Communities of the Arab World as Portrayed in the Documents of the Cairo Geniza*, 4 vols., University of California Press, 1966, ff.

GOLDBERG, H. E., "The Mimuna and the Minority Status of Moroccan Jews," *Ethnology*, 17, 1978, no. 1, pp. 75–88.

GREVIN, Emmanuel, *Djerba, l'île heureuse, et le Sud tunisien*, Paris, 1937.

HACOHEN, Moshe Khalfon, *Brith Kehuna*, 4 vols., Jerba, 1941–1951.

HACOHEN, Moshe Khalfon (ed.), *Ma'assei Beth Din,* Jerba, n.d.

HACOHEN, Shushan, *Pelei Sadiqim*, Jerba, 1930.

HACOHEN, Shushan, *Mamekhet Kohanim*, Jerusalem, n.d.

HADDAD, Boaz, *Jerba Yehudit*, Jerusalem, 1978.

HADDAD, Efraim, *Shorashim bi-Yehadut Tunisia*, Beersheva, 1978.

HIRSCHBERG, H. Z., *A History of the Jews in North Africa*, vol. 1, Leiden, 1974.

AL-IDRISI, *Description de l'Afrique et de l'Espagne par Edrisi*, ed., and trans. R. Dozy and M. J. de Goeje, Leiden, 1866.

LANFREDUCCI and Bosio, "Costa e dicorsi di Barberia (1587)," *Revue Africaine*, vol. 66, 1925.

MADAR, Messiad, *Sha'arei Tahara*, Jerba, 1963.

MONCHICOURT, Charles, "L'expédition espagnole de 1560 contre l'île de Djerba," *Revue Tunisienne*, 1913 and 1914.

MONTEIL, Vincent, "Les Juifs d'Ifran (Anti-Atlas marocain)," *Hespéris*, 1948, XXXV, ler-2e trim., pp. 151—162.

PINKERFELD Jacob, "Un témoignage du passé en voie de disparition: les synagogues de la région de Djerba," *Cahiers de Byrsa*, 1957, VII, pp. 127—188.

ROY, Bruno, *Contribution à l'étude des communautés juives du sud-est de la Tunisie*, Thèse polycopiée, Monpellier, 1969.

SEBAG, Paul, "Les Juifs de Tunis au XIXe siècle, d'après Benjamin II," *Cahiers de Tunisie*, no. 28, vol. 7, 1959.
SLOUSCHZ, Nahum

no. 28, vol. 7, 1959.

SLOUSCHZ, Nahum, *Ha-i Peli*, Tel Aviv, 1957.

SLOUSCHZ, Nahum, *The Jews of North Africa*, Philadelphia, 1927.

SLOUSCHZ, Nahum, *Un voyage d'études juives en Afrique*, Paris, 1909.

TLATLI, Salah-Eddine, *Djerba l'île des Lotophages*, Tunis, 1967.

ZAFRANI, Haim, *Les Juifs du Maroc. Vie Sociale, économique et religieuse. Ètude de Taqqanot et Responsa*, Paris, 1972.

Glossary

a = Arabic word   h = Hebrew word

Bar mitzva	h	Ceremony by which an adolescent boy reaches religious majority at age 13.
Beth Din	h	Rabbinic court.
Bimah	h	Raised platform in the center of the synagogue.
Bint 'amm	a	Daughter of the paternal uncle. The bint 'amm is the preferred bride in traditional Arab marriage customs.
Chechia	a	Round felt cap worn by men.
Dar	a	House, designating the building and the extended family in it.
Dayyan	h	Rabbinic judge
Delet	h	Door
Delwaji	a	Bucket-maker.
Dhimmi	a	A non-Muslim subject of a Muslim country, protected by the dhimma.
Drash	h	Homily, sermon.
'Eruv	h	On the Sabbath, Jews are not allowed to transport objects beyond the domestic space. The 'eruv, usually a wire strung around a town or city, converts the entire enclosed space into a licit area for carrying objects on the Sabbath.
Fidyun	h	The *pidyon ha-ben*, pronounced fidyun in Jerba, is the ceremony of redeeming the first born child, if it is male, from a kohen for the equivalent of 5 shekels.
Fouta	a	A large piece of silk material in which women wrap themselves when they leave their homes.
Galut	h	Exile, diaspora.
Geniza (Cairo)	h	A cache of documents and papers dating from the 10th century onwards, found in the synagogue of Old Cairo.
Ghaba	a	Forest, countryside.
Ghriba	a	Strange, solitary, marvelous.
Goy (pl. goyyim)	h	Non-Jew.
Haggada	h	Text read at the Passover seder.
Halakha	h	The body of Jewish religous law.
Halal	a	Licit, permissible, the opposite of *haram*, forbidden.
Hanukka	h	A holiday celebrated for 8 days beginning with 25th of Kislev to commemorate the reconsecration of the Temple.
Hallel	h	Prayer composed in the main of selections from the Psalms and recited on the major festivals.
Haram	a	Forbidden, sacred, opposite of *halal.*
Heikhal	h	Cabinet which holds the scrolls of the Torah.
Hillula	h	Literally, wedding, but used to designate the anniversary of the death of holy men of the past.
'Inara	h	Local pronunciation of the Hebrew word *'ayn hara'* — evil eye.
Isti'mar	a	Domination, imperialism.
Jizya	a	Poll-tax to be levied on the dhimmis according to Islamic religious law.
Kiddush	h	A prayer (usually over wine) pronounced before Sabbath and holiday meals.
Khalkhal	a	Silver or gold ankle bracelet.
Kohen (pl. Kohanim)	h	Member of the priestly caste of descendants of Aaron, brother of Moses.

Kol Nidre	h	Opening prayer of the Yom Kippur service.
Ktav sefardi	h	Local, cursive Hebrew writing in which the alphabet differs from that of standard Hebrew.
Lulav (pl. lulavim)	h	Frond of a palm tree, used in the ceremonies of the festival of Succoth.
Ma'ariv	h	Evening prayer service.
Menara	a	Candelabrum
Menzel	a	Traditional Jerban residence, usually a square structure built around a courtyard with angled towers and situated in the open countryside.
Mezuza (pl. mezuzot)	h	A piece of parchment with text of Deuteronomy VI, 4-9 and XI, 3-21, folded and attached to the doorposts of houses and rooms.
Mikveh	h	Ritual bath.
Minha	h	Late afternoon prayer.
Minhag	h	Custom.
Mitzva (pl. mitzvot)	h	Commandment prescribed by Jewish religious law; a good deed.
Mohel	h	Person qualified to perform circumcisions according to the prescriptions of the law.
Nul	a	Weaving workshop.
Piyyut (pl. piyyutim)	h	Poem, usually of a liturgical nature.
Qahal	h	Community
Qina	h	Dirge, poems of mourning read on the 9th of Av and during the weeks preceding.
Responsum		Juridical consultation written in response to questions on points in rabbinic law. The Jewish counterpart of the Islamic *fatwa*.
Rosh hodesh	h	First day of the Jewish lunar month, i.e., the new moon.
Rosh ha-Shanah	h	New Year.
Seder	h	The ritual meal of the first two nights of Passover; in Jerba and in other parts of North Africa it also refers to the festive meals of the New Year.
Shaharit	h	The morning prayer.
Shavu'oth	h	Literally: weeks. Festival commemorating the receipt of the law by Moses on Mt. Sinai, celebrated seven weeks after Passover.
Shofar	h	A ram's horn sounded in the ritual of the New Year and Yom Kippur; and in Jerba, every Friday afternoon to announce the advent of the Sabbath.
Shohet	h	Ritual slaughterer; person qualified to slaughter animals according to the requirements of rabbinic law.
Shulhan 'Arukh	h	Codification of rabbinic law compiled by Joseph Caro in Palestine in the 16th century.
Simhat Torah	h	Festival of the Torah, marking the completion of the annual cycle of the reading of the Torah.
Sla	a	Synagogue.
Succoth	h	Festival of Booths, Tabernacles.
Suq	a	Market.
Ta'rovet	h	Mixture of genres.
Tbila	h	Immersion in a ritual bath (mikveh)
Tefilin	h	Phylacteries.
Tfina arisha	a	The traditional dish for the lunch meal on Saturday.
Yeshiva (pl. yeshivot)	h	Rabbinical academy; in Jerba it designates the religious school for boys.
Ziyara	a	Pilgrimage to the tomb of a marabout.
Zohar	h	The Book of Splendor, attributed to Rabbi Shim'on bar Yohai of the 2nd century A.D. Scholars believe that it was actually composed in 13th century Spain. It forms the basis of kabbalistic mysticism.